Communicative Methodology
in Language Teaching

CAMBRIDGE LANGUAGE TEACHING LIBRARY
A series of authoritative books on subjects of central importance for all
language teachers.

In this series:

Communicative Methodology in Language Teaching

The roles of fluency
and accuracy

Christopher Brumfit

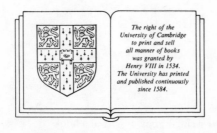

The right of the
University of Cambridge
to print and sell
all manner of books
was granted by
Henry VIII in 1534.
The University has printed
and published continuously
since 1584.

Cambridge University Press
Cambridge
London   New York   New Rochelle
Melbourne   Sydney

Published by the Press Syndicate of the University of Cambridge
The Pitt Building, Trumpington Street, Cambridge CB2 1RP
32 East 57th Street, New York, NY 10022, USA
10 Stamford Road, Oakleigh, Melbourne 3166, Australia

© Cambridge University Press 1984

First published 1984
Third printing 1987

Printed in Great Britain
at the University Press, Cambridge

Library of Congress catalogue card number: 83–26239

British Library cataloguing in publication data

Brumfit, C.J.
Communicative methodology in language
teaching. – (Cambridge language teaching
library)
1. Languages, Modern – Study and teaching
I. Title
418'.007   PB35

ISBN 0 521 26423 5 hard covers
ISBN 0 521 26968 7 paperback

WD

For Simon

In what sense, we may well ask, do men 'make' their history? Conscious effort, deliberate attempts to explain the world to oneself, to discover oneself in it, to obtain from it what one needs and wants, to adapt means to ends, to express one's vision or describe what one sees or feels or thinks, individually or collectively – understanding, communication, creation – all these could be described as kinds of doing and making. But this omits too much: unconscious and irrational 'drives', which even the most developed and trained psychological methods cannot guarantee to lay bare; the unintended and unforeseen consequences of our acts, which we cannot be said to have 'made' if making entails intention; the play of accident; the entire natural world by interaction with which we live and function, which remains opaque inasmuch as it is not, *ex hypothesi*, the work of our hands or minds; since we do not 'make' this, how can any-thing it possesses be grasped as *verum*? How can there be a *scienza* of such an amalgam?

Isaiah Berlin: Vico's Concept of Knowledge
(Berlin, 1980: 115)

Contents

Preface

This book derives from my Ph.D. thesis, 'The Basis of a Communicative Methodology in Language Teaching', presented at the University of London in January 1983. A large number of changes have been made, some quite major and many minor, in order to make it more suitable for a wider audience.

I had to make an important decision about the academic paraphernalia, references and footnotes, which attach themselves to theses. Many of these I have cut, but it seems unfair in a work which is deliberately synthesising educational, philosophical and linguistic scholarship to prevent readers from following up arguments and checking their own agreement with my interpretations. Consequently, I have retained enough scholarly apparatus to enable critics to attack me. In spite of the title, much of this book is a general argument, and illustration of that argument, about the nature and justification of research in teaching methodology. This argument can only be justified by reference to the earlier arguments and research from which it springs – so the references and notes are there, it is hoped unobtrusively, for those who wish to exploit them.

CJB
August 1983

Acknowledgements

The arguments on which this study is based have been conducted over a long period with many people, who may well not recognise their own contributions, let alone agree with the final position adopted.

Selection of those to mention is always invidious, especially when colleagues and students have been so generous with their time. I am conscious, however, of particular debts in the argument offered here to the following: Brian Abbs, Dick Allwright, Roy Boardman, Geoffrey Broughton, Ken Cripwell, Patrick Early, Rod Ellis, Roger Flavell, Roger Hawkey, Peter Hill, Keith Johnson, Josie Levine, Alan Maley, John Munby, John Norrish, Anita Pincas, Ken Reeder, Harold Rosen, Richard Rossner, Earl Stevick, Peter Strevens and Monica Vincent.

I am also grateful to N.S. Prabhu for permission to make use of Bangalore material, as well as for much stimulating discussion.

The Modern Language Centre of Ontario Institute for Studies in Education gave me facilities while I was writing this study, and I benefited greatly from their library and support services, and from discussions with, among others, Patrick Allen, Michael Canale, Maria Fröhlich, and Merrill Swain. I was especially grateful for the time and generous consideration offered by David Stern.

I am most grateful to my editor, Alison Baxter, from whom I have received a vast amount of help in clarifying both my ideas and the text.

Finally I have simultaneous personal and professional acknowledgements to make, on the one hand to Henry Widdowson, whose discussion and moral support have both been indispensable, and on the other to my wife and son, who have provided me with evidence, scepticism, suggestion and security in approximately equal measures.

Introduction: what this book stands for

This study is an investigation of ideas in an area which is unclearly defined as a field for research: teaching methodology. Administratively, it is classed as a sub-branch of education, but it is clear that educational disciplines alone cannot provide an adequate base for the examination of principles in the teaching of a particular subject. Nor, it is argued here, can the linguistic sciences alone provide a basis for the teaching of languages, for the interaction of language with, on the one hand, personal needs of language users and, on the other, institutional constraints of the users' setting will make an autonomous, linguistic theory of performance impossible. The researcher in this area thus has two choices available. One is to reject this argument, limit the field, and idealise the data, so that it becomes manageable in terms of criteria appropriate to one of the agreed disciplines: linguistics, psychology, or sociology. The other is to remain in the same position as the practising teacher, but to try to examine that position as critically as possible. This choice entails accepting three conditions, all of which make discussion in methodology particularly difficult:

i)   generalisations and principles must be capable of being related directly to existing teaching conditions, including teachers as they actually are, institutions as they actually are, and resources as they actually are;

ii) information, principles, metaphors and (to use the vogue term) 'insights' will be drawn from a whole range of different sources and integrated into some sort of coherent position which is directly translatable into classroom behaviour;

iii) perceptions must reflect the position of the teacher in the classroom – that is to say that they must in the end refer to the process of intervening in the lives of others in order to assist desirable changes of behaviour.

We expect all teachers, implicitly through the ways in which we train them, to accept these conditions in their professional self-consciousness; but most research in education imitates research in other disciplines, differing only in the context or subject matter of the study. In this study, we are attempting to perform exactly the same kind of conceptualising task that we demand of language teachers, but at a higher level of abstraction. This inevitably creates certain problems.

The desire to remain closely in touch with conditions as they actually are leads to caution and perhaps a lack of speculative excitement. But at the same time, we cannot allow all discussion of teaching to ignore the rules that are imposed on teachers by the nature of their positions as teachers. Without denying the value of idealised constructs and divergent thinking unconstrained by the fetters of immediate responsibility, we need also to demonstrate and practise the art of assessing the value for teaching of the work in areas that are less constrained.

The process of drawing upon research findings, theoretical constructs, and practical suggestions from a wide range of potentially relevant sciences inevitably results in major risks of error. We shall be dependent on secondary sources for some, at least, of our observations; and we can master some disciplines only at the expense of others, or of our contact with the teaching in the service of which the interdisciplinary exercise is being performed. Synthesis may be seen simply as a derivative activity, unsuitable for serious research pretensions, and the difficulties arising from an attempt to be interdisciplinary may be seen as resulting from a refusal to focus sharply on clearly identifiable problems. Yet we cannot afford to leave all questions of how to synthesise research conclusions to teachers actually working in classrooms, for – more often than not – they lack expertise, training, and above all, time for such activity. Furthermore, the frequently-desired integration of theory and practice requires illustrations of the process of doing this at all levels. It is no service to the profession if all those who are theoretically minded address themselves exclusively to questions that can be answered within the frameworks of existing disciplines. Particularly, in departments of teaching methods, it is essential that we attempt to examine precisely the kinds of questions that we expect our students to examine. If we do not do this, however badly, we shall be leaving the most difficult problems to those who have least time, facilities, or inclination to explore them.

Working from the position of the teacher means that there is an inevitable antagonism between many research approaches and that which we have adopted here. This is partly because research is often descriptive, either looking at the teacher from outside (a position inappropriate for teachers attempting to improve their own performance), or looking at learners, or language, or classrooms with non-interventionist intentions. This does not prevent the teacher from making use of such data, of course, but it does mean that insofar as teachers appear in research studies they are often portrayed over-simply or unsympathetically, either because the teacher's function may be peripheral to the main object of the study, or because researchers have little fully committed experience of teaching and misconstrue its nature and its function. But again, this is all the more reason why we should not refuse to address ourselves to research from the teacher's perspective.

Ultimately, this is a study based on personal experience of teaching, which is thus, in retrospect, necessarily systematised and idealised. From that experience, theory, observation, speculation, and practice have been examined in order to attempt to clarify the principles underlying the experience. The first chapter tries to explore the status of such principles and the nature of our understanding of teaching. The difficulty lies in the tension between our recognition of teaching as primarily a product of the relationship between human beings, and the view, tacitly supported by the structure of the educational hierarchy and the design of teacher training, that it is some kind of applied science. It will be argued in this study that there is no necessary antagonism between these two positions, but a research tradition that emphasizes the latter at the expense of the former will only exacerbate the tension.

This is a study, then, that attempts to be interdisciplinary and integrative, even if that means that it cannot operate within the work of any single discipline. It concerns itself with the needs of normal state educational systems, even when these may limit the possibilities of educational innovation. And it examines language-teaching principles from the point of view of teachers who, as a profession, are committed to positive intervention in the lives of other people. Above all, it is an attempt to devise a simple conceptual framework for the whole of language teaching, within which the needs of specific courses can be worked out according to the requirements of local conditions.

1 Research methodology, teaching methodology, and educational values

This book operates simultaneously in the fields of education and applied linguistics. Its initial impetus is educational: the language-teaching profession has developed over the last seventy years or so a mass of experience backed up to varying degrees by research, but there often appears to be a conflict between the art of teaching and the science of understanding the nature of language and the nature of teaching. This book attempts to express a view of language teaching, within a general educational framework, which is both coherent scientifically and philosophically, and compatible with the common-sense apprehensions of teachers whose experience and temperament lead them to commitment to *language teaching*, but not to a particular concern with scientific or philosophical insights. In part, therefore, this argument may equally apply to the teaching of any subject, for it is concerned with the relationship between principle and practice, or between what can be analysed and what is experienced. In this sense I am defining the role of teaching methodology in relation to both theory and practice, and physics or history teachers will recognise the difficulties just as much as language specialists.

Since, however, my particular concern is with language teaching, much of the argument will develop out of a view of the nature of language. Necessarily, then, we shall have to examine various implications of linguistic theories for the classroom. But we shall not consider these in isolation, for no real-world problem will be solved by the direct application of linguistic models, for these are idealised constructs which will inevitably be distorted as they come into contact with all the non-linguistic factors that also influence our activities as human beings.

Even though this first chapter is only indirectly related to language teaching, it is a very important chapter for my argument. Later in the book I shall be exploring appropriate teaching procedures for language teaching to non-native speakers. But I shall not be regarding this exploration as primarily 'scientific' nor as largely 'intuitive'; instead, I shall argue that methodological innovation in teaching is a kind of social intervention which cannot be precisely measured or controlled, though it can (and must) be monitored. Since there are strong forces in education which would like to concentrate on what is measurable and provable, and equally strong opponents who resent attacks on their instinctive classroom improvisation and creativity, the adoption of a middle position needs to be justified.

I shall look briefly, then, at key questions on the nature of scientific understanding. In the first section of this chapter, some key problems in the exploration of human behaviour will be examined. In the second, these problems will be related explicitly to issues in teaching methodology. In the third, we shall address ourselves more directly to problems in language-teaching methodology.

1.1 Science, human science, and non-science

Teaching is an activity which is performed, directly or indirectly, by human beings on human beings. Consequently, everyone who writes about it is a potential teacher or pupil. For this reason alone there will be influences on our assessments of what we observe in teaching which will be quite different from those on our observations of non-human activities. Furthermore, in practice those who write on teaching are more likely to bring to bear 'personal knowledge' (Polyani, 1958) of a fairly direct kind than those who write on some other aspects of human behaviour – for example, anthropologists working in a culture different from their own.

Kinds of knowledge

One of the most important problems posed by the recognition of 'personal knowledge' is that of establishing the status of the various different ways of knowing about something. One major distinction of this kind was much discussed in the late nineteenth century when the social sciences were being established as legitimate areas of study, though it has been ignored in more recent behaviouralist approaches to social sciences. In work leading up to his *Ideas about a Descriptive and Analytical Psychology* in 1894, Dilthey developed a distinction between *verstehen* (to understand) and *erleben* (to experience), which is crucial in any discussion of academic work on teaching methodology. He was primarily concerned with differentiating between the natural and social sciences, but what he has to say has a direct bearing on the experience of teachers who have become teacher trainers, or methodologists.

We do not show ourselves genuine disciples of the great scientific thinkers simply by transferring their methods to our sphere; we must adjust our knowledge to the nature of our subject-matter and thus treat it as the scientists treat theirs. We conquer nature by submitting to it. The human studies differ from the sciences because the latter deal with facts which present themselves to consciousness as external and separate phenomena, while the former deal with the living connections of reality experienced in the mind. It follows that the sciences arrive at connections within nature through inferences by means of a combination of hypotheses while the human sciences are based on directly given mental connections. We explain nature but we understand mental life . . . The experience of the whole context comes first; only later do we understand its individual parts.

(Dilthey, 1894, cited from Dilthey, 1976: 89)

Although much recent thinking on the interaction between perception and understanding (for example, Popper and Eccles, 1977) would question the account of scientific understanding given here, the distinction as made by Dilthey does emphasize the unique character of an investigation of human activity carried out by another human being.

One way of accepting the role of experience is to see it as authenticating the object of study. Winch claims

that a historian or sociologist of religion must himself have some religious feeling if he is to make sense of the religious movement he is studying and understand the considerations which govern the lives of its participants. A historian of art must have some aesthetic sense if he is to understand the problems confronting the artists of his period; and without this he will have left out of his account precisely what would have made it a history of *art*, as opposed to a rather puzzling external account of certain motions which certain people have been perceived to go through.

(Winch, 1958: 88)

It may be objected, though, that part of the process of understanding art or religion depends on our being able to see them from the outside as 'certain motions'; indeed, this is the principle of 'making strange' identified by Soviet formalist literary critics as one source of literary understanding (Bayley, 1966: 103–4; Hawkes, 1977: 62–6). There is no reason to produce an analysis for someone who already has understanding, so the process of analysing must demand some ability to stand outside the object; but an analysis which shows no sign of understanding the experience risks mistaking the function of the experience and therefore misinterpreting its characteristics.

It is possible, however, to make a stronger claim for experience, a claim which goes back at least as far as Vico, who reacted strongly to what he perceived as the excessively cognitive emphasis of Descartes. Berlin characterises this as follows:

It is a knowing founded on memory or imagination . . . This is the sort of knowing which participants in an activity claim to possess as against mere observers; the knowledge of the actors, as against that of the audience, of the 'inside' story as opposed to that obtained from some 'outside' vantage point; knowledge by 'direct acquaintance' with my 'inner' states or by sympathetic insight into those of others, which may be obtained by a high degree of imaginative power; the knowledge that is involved when a work of the imagination or of social diagnosis or a work of criticism or scholarship or history is described not as correct or incorrect, skilful or inept, a success or a failure, but as profound or shallow, realistic or unrealistic, perceptive or stupid, alive or dead. What this capacity is, the part that it plays in the understanding of the simplest communication addressed by one sentient creature to another, and *a fortiori* in the creation of adequate vehicles of expression, of criticism, above all in the recovery of the past not as a collection of factual beads strung on a chronicler's string (or of 'ideas', arguments, works of art, similarly treated by the taxonomists and antiquaries of the humanities), but as a possible world, a society which could have had such characteristics whether it had precisely these or not – the nature of this kind of knowing is Vico's central topic.

(Berlin, 1980: 117)

And to claim that this paragraph demonstrates a commitment on the part of Berlin in excess of that required by the need to describe Vico's position is to make a claim, as a reader, to precisely the kind of knowledge being referred to. The validity of this claim depends on readers of this text agreeing with my assessment of Berlin's involvement with Vico's ideas.[1]* We are thus talking about a kind of understanding which is fundamental to the process of human communication, and which will be considered in more detail in Chapter 2.

For the moment, though, it is enough to note that there is a strong intellectual tradition for the assertion that not only do we have:

        1   knowledge that . . .
and   2   knowledge how to . . .
but also 3   knowledge of what it is to . . .

'Knowledge of what it is to be a language teacher' has a legitimate claim to be considered in methodological discussion, as it is expressed through the accumulated professional wisdom, and folly, of teachers. Language-teaching tradition, by the mere fact of its existence as tradition, has to be seen in part as knowledge about language teaching. To claim this is not to argue for an uncritical acceptance of tradition, nor that traditions are not shaped in part by laziness or outmoded assumptions; it is to recognise that we cannot understand teaching methodology by simply considering language and the processes of teaching from the outside.

Natural and human sciences

Nevertheless, a claim that we should take account of understanding through experience does not resolve the problem of relations between natural and human sciences. The most attractive early solution of this problem was to claim that in principle human behaviour could eventually be converted to natural science, rather as Mill, in the classic statement of

---

*Notes will be found on pages 137–44.

the inductive approach to scientific method, refers to the problems of tides, or of meteorology.

Take, for instance, the most familiar class of meteorological phenomena, those of rain and sunshine. Scientific inquiry has not yet succeeded in ascertaining the order of antecedence and consequence among these phenomena, so as to be able, at least in our regions of the earth, to predict them with certainty or even with any high degree of probability. Yet no one doubts that the phenomena depend on laws, and that these must be derivative laws resulting from known ultimate laws, those of heat, electricity, vaporisation, and elastic fluids.

(Mill, 1843: 552)

And Mill later claims:

The science of human nature is of this description. It falls far short of the standard of exactness now realised in Astronomy; but there is no reason that it should not be as much a science as Tidology is . . .

(Mill, 1843: 553)

Such a view leads directly to attempts to set up a model of language behaviour in which the language can in principle be predicted by a precise specification of the conditions leading to its use (Skinner, 1957), or to quantify the complexities of human social behaviour (Simon, 1957).

But, as several commentators have pointed out, Mill confuses the process of discovery with the process of proof,[2] although at least one philosopher (Whewell, 1840) had clearly distinguished the two processes before the publication of Mill's *A System of Logic*. Consequently, even his account of discovery in natural sciences can be questioned, while the logical status of generalisations from evidence has been severely undercut by Popper, to whose work we shall now turn.

Popper's work is of particular relevance to educational research, because it substitutes for the notion of acquiring firm knowledge by inductive reasoning that of the temporary solution of problems by formulating appropriate falsifiable statements. Such statements have only provisional status because, in Popper's view, there can be no proof of a scientific statement: such statements can be falsified by one piece of counter evidence, but we shall not be able to predict that such counter evidence is never likely to appear. Scientific statements can be tested, however, by consistent attempts to refute them (Popper, 1934, 1963, 1972; see also Magee, 1973). Popper recounts how he originally developed his position by worrying about the status of theories, such as the psycho-analytic proposals current in Vienna in 1919–20. Compared with Marxism, which – because it made predictions – was refutable and, indeed, refuted by subsequent events, or Einstein, who made predictions which were not refuted, psycho-analytic theories posed a different problem.

They were simply non-testable, irrefutable. There was no conceivable human behaviour which could contradict them. This does not mean that Freud and Adler were not seeing certain things correctly: I personally do not doubt that much of what they say is of considerable importance, and may well play its part one day in a psychological science which is testable. But it does mean that those 'clinical observations' which analysts naïvely believe confirm their theory cannot do this any more than the daily confirmation which astrologers find in their practice.

(Popper, 1963: 37–8)

Many casual claims in education are similarly irrefutable. For example, it is frequently maintained that teaching will be effective so long as the relationship between class and teacher is satisfactory. While such a comment may be helpful to a trainee teacher (as Popper indicates, non-falsifiable statements are not necessarily useless), it cannot as it stands be used as a basis for a serious analysis of classroom behaviour.

Nonetheless, Popper does give us the basis for a consideration of human sciences on the same principles as natural sciences, for, by emphasising problem solving, he is able to introduce the principle of appropriate toleration of uncertainty. A statement should be precise enough to enable it to be falsified in terms of the problem it is devised to solve. 'How many inches high must a little sand-hill be in order to be called "sand-dune"? How quickly must the air move in order to be called "wind"?' he asks (Popper, 1945, Vol. 2: 19). This is part of an argument against the demand for 'scientific precision' on the grounds that precision is only useful in relation to a particular problem which needs solving. The prime task of a scientist, then, is to state problems clearly enough for them to be tested, so that the problem statements thus lay themselves open to falsification. The whole point about scientific knowledge, Popper claims, is that it is not a series of 'facts' but a series of provisional statements, publicly available for testing and principled modification (Popper, 1972: 108). The precise methodology of testing, and the criteria for falsification, will vary according to the nature of the problem being addressed. Hence, even issues which involve the making of value judgements, such as decisions over social policy, including education, may be treated as hypotheses, to be adjusted according to publicly acknowledged criteria of success or failure – providing they have been precisely formulated in test-able terms. The extent to which issues in teaching methodology can be addressed thus is a topic that we shall return to.

Before we leave Popper's work, however, it is worth referring to one characteristic which has not been greatly emphasized. That is the simi-larity between the research process, as he describes it, and normal linguis-tic behaviour. His view of science is essentially a social view in which the new researcher is instructed to 'study the *problem situation* of the day' (Popper, 1963: 129) and to develop constructs by interaction with others who are interested in the same areas. Furthermore, the scientific knowledge of the time, or provisional solutions, are currently agreed conventions on the basis of which currently interesting problems may be investigated – but they are necessarily negotiable because each time a proposed solution fails *any* new proposal may become a candidate for further refinement and testing. The procedure rests on an assumption of free creativity modified by conventional adjustments in the process of human interaction.[3] As we shall see in Chapter 2, this corresponds closely with current views on the nature of linguistic behaviour.

We have, then, a view of science which both allows a place for human action, and which can incorporate the instinct or experiential understanding of the practitioner, as described by Berlin (1980) and Winch (1958) above. The issue of the source of the understanding becomes unimportant, so long as the understanding is publicly formulated and explicitly turned into testable statements. In this view, substantive errors – false hypotheses – are forgivable (even, if they prove useful, commendable); but the heinous offence is a refusal to come out and fight in the open. Medawar, reviewing Koestler's *The Act of Creation* (Koestler, 1964) defines it thus:

> But certain rules of scientific manners must be observed no matter what form the account of a scientific theory may take. One must mention (if only to dismiss with contempt) other, alternative explanations of the matters one is dealing with; and one must discuss (if only to prove them groundless) some of the objections that are likely to be raised against one's theories by the ignorant or ill-disposed.
>
> (Medawar, 1967: 91)

And this is a position which need not rest on a Popperian epistemology. Hirst arrives at a similar position as a result of an analysis, for explicitly educational purposes, not of scientific procedures, but of forms of knowledge. He writes:

> I see no grounds for accepting that being rational in any sphere is a matter of adherence to a set of principles that are of their character invariant, nor do I see why formal systems of relations of a mathematical kind should be regarded as providing any necessary ideal of rationality against which all other forms must be assessed. Being rational I see rather as a way of developing conceptual schemes by means of public language in which words are related to our form of life, so that we make objective judgements in relation to some aspect of that form of life. The precise character of those schemes is a matter of investigation, not something that can be laid down in advance, in terms of some ideal, no matter how successful or attractive one particular scheme may be. How far such schemes do as a matter of fact have an invariant structure, is a question for research. Intelligibility in public language and objectivity of judgement would seem to be the demands of reason.
>
> (Hirst, 1974: 92–3)

But intelligibility in public language does presuppose some consensus on appropriate frames of reference for particular fields of discourse, and this implies the establishment of more or less coherent descriptive systems. As long as these are regarded as useful conventions, they pose little problem, but if they are stabilised as some form of 'truth' they become non-negotiable and hence irrefutable and non-scientific.

We may conclude this section, then, by isolating four points central to our argument:

1 understanding, whether of the natural or human world, may be tentatively arrived at through any kind of experience or intuition;
2 such understanding can be claimed as scientific only in relation to specific problems to be solved;
3 the clear specification of the problem should lead to tentative solutions which need to be expressed precisely enough to be testable;
4 the process of testing and assessment should be carried out publicly, with every effort being made to falsify claims.

The last two points will be examined more closely in the next section, and in the rest of this chapter we shall be considering the extent to which investigation and discussion of teaching methodology can fit into this framework.

1.2   Social science and the methodology of teaching

The kinds of problem that Popper had in mind early in his career were clearly intellectual problems. The kinds of problem that teachers are habitually confronted with are far more practical, and are usually expressed in terms which are too vague to be immediately testable. Typical examples might be:

a) what will be the effect on my class if I use textbook X rather than textbook Y?
b) what are the best procedures for correcting mistakes?
c) what is the optimal size of class?

None of these problems can be addressed until a situation is specified much more closely, because all of them involve generalisations which are so broad as to demand answers at the level of maxims ('If you wish your class to thrive, don't go over twenty-five') rather than of analysis.

Since Popper moved more and more towards a problem-solving procedure of wider application, it is worth asking what kinds of answer would be appropriate in principle for questions involving human relations. Some scholars (for example, Hempel, 1962; Easton, 1965) have argued for a continuity between pure and applied science which goes back more to the inductive tradition of Mill than to that of Popper. Hempel, particularly, has argued that the modes of explanation in natural science and in history (seen as an example of a human science) are essentially the same, except that the human sciences, while empirically based, are concerned with probability rather than with certainty (Hempel, in Colodny, 1962, chap. 1). It is certainly unlikely that even a more precise definition of the teaching problems listed above would be capable of a solution in any except crudely probabilistic terms.

But a discussion of probabilities raises crucial questions of the relationship between experimental or observed data and the situations to which the results will be applied. It may be true, as Hempel's discussion of a text on Luther and indulgences shows, that historians use notions of probability for explanatory purposes, but this has not led them to make the kind of predictions demanded by Popper of a scientific theory. The difficult question, in social situations, is: When are two situations examples of the same phenomenon? This question arises whenever we try to generalise from specific experimental data. In the field of social psychology – reasonably close to that of classroom interaction – there are frequent problems of this kind. Hinde (1979: 254–5) refers, for example, to attempts to measure the amount of conflict in a relationship. Several studies investigated different aspects of the problem, but we shall take one as an example. Ravich and Wyden (1974) claim to detect a pattern of behaviour in a game in which married couples operate a train and a gate each on a pattern of electric train tracks. The trains may collide or avoid each other at the gates, and imaginary pennies can be won by performing effectively in relation to time. Ravich and Wyden claim that the couples develop a measurable pattern of behaviour, in terms of relations like dominant–submissive, co-operative, competitive, and combinations of these, and 60 per cent of couples fall into one of the three major categories. Clearly, such studies do shed light on the processes of co-operation and conflict in the performance of given (and, we should note, laboratory-based) tasks. But we cannot usefully claim that the principles involved will extrapolate to the particularities of even these subjects' relationships, which must be dependent on conditions of their lives together, memories of their past experiences of each other, and the humdrum characteristics of contingent life. The translation from laboratory interaction to marital interaction – or, even more, to generalisations about interpersonal interaction as a social phenomenon – seems misconceived.[4]

We may want to argue, on the basis of this and similar experimental evidence, combined with arguments about the limits of historical prediction, that explanation in social terms is only possible with hindsight. However, we cannot avoid a responsibility for acting according to predictions about the effects of our actions, even if we wish to. This is not the place to argue a fully-fledged political philosophy, but it must be recognised that the results of refusing to take responsibility for the future, either on the grounds that it is predetermined or that it cannot be affected by planning, is to hand over to those who are less scrupulous. We have to act *as if* we can take principled decisions, *but* we have to insist on sensitive feedback mechanisms, either formal or informal, to enable us to adjust to the variations and failures in our predictions.

Such a view will lead us to be cautious about the predictive value of the behaviouralist tradition, as seen, for example, in Easton's arguments. He summarises the main features of the tradition under eight major headings:

1 regularities in behaviour;
2 verification of generalisations;
3 techniques for acquiring and interpreting data needing to be refined and constantly analysed;
4 quantification of data where appropriate;
5 values to be separated from 'empirical explanation';
6 systematisation of research;
7 pure science preceding application;
8 integration of various disciplines inevitable when dealing with the human situation.

(Easton, 1965: 7)

Such an approach has many attractions as a basis for description with a close relationship to the procedures of the natural sciences. But there is no way in which these procedures can in themselves make the jump from description to prediction without coming into conflict with the features of the human mind outlined in the discussion of Vico at the beginning of this chapter. Such an argument, like that commonly used against the scientific standing of opinion polls and psephology (Ions, 1977, chap. VII), prevents us accepting any human science as crudely predictive.[5]

One further attempt to deal with the human sciences should be mentioned, if only because it has been influential in discussions of educational issues. Hirst (1974: 86–7) makes a clear distinction between the parts of sociology and psychology which are 'strictly of the physical science variety', and those which are concerned with 'explanations of human behaviour in terms of intentions, will, hopes, beliefs, etc.' He argues that 'the concepts, logical structure and truth criteria of propositions of this latter kind are . . . different from, and not reducible to, those of the former kind'. The consequence of this is that he would regard history and the social sciences as hybrid subjects, concerned with forms of knowledge of logically different kinds within the same subject. This distinction does not help our argument here, though it may reinforce despair, but it does perhaps indicate one of the problems in translating from the laboratory or the empirical data base to prediction. It is difficult to imagine a classroom, or any other social or political setting, in which human intentions, wills, hopes, and beliefs were not important factors in what happened, but such factors cannot appear in a behaviouralist description.

The nature of teaching

So far we have assumed that an investigation of the methodology of teaching must be undertaken as part of a 'human science'. It is time now, though, to look more closely at the concept of teaching, in order to relate it both to our earlier discussion of the investigation of human behaviour and to the characteristics of language activity, which will be analysed later. There is of course a massive literature on this topic, and it is unnecessary for our purposes to try to be exhaustive, but there are nonetheless a number of important points of clarification which need to be made.

Hirst, in a paper entitled 'What is teaching?' (1974: 101–15), starts by distinguishing teaching, the enterprise, which includes such activities as calling registers and opening windows, from the process of teaching itself, and goes on to point out that it is a 'polymorphous activity', which can in principle include any behaviour. The only useful way of defining it, he concludes, is in terms of its purpose – to cause learning – though he points out that it is sometimes used with an implication of success as well as purpose, as in 'He taught me to ride a bicycle'. Langford makes similar points in emphasizing that 'teaching is not the name of a method of doing anything' (Langford, 1968: 124), and rather earlier Scheffler (1960: 76) had drawn up a convenient paradigm on the basis of three distinctions:

a)   X tells Y that . . .   c)   X tells Y to . . .
b)   X teaches Y that . . .   d)   X teaches Y to . . .
      e)   X tells Y how to . . .
      f)   X teaches Y how to . . .

As we shall see when we look more closely at language teaching, these three distinctions do not exhaust the possible relationships between teachers and pupils, but they do illustrate the three most discussed aspects of teaching: knowledge (b), attitude (d), and skill (f) – a division which corresponds to that used in the influential Bloom taxonomy (Bloom, 1956). In addition, the 'tell/teach' distinction is convenient in its illustration of the emphasis for the teacher on the reaction of the learner.

If teaching is an attempt to cause somebody else to change, then a clear specification of the desired change, and some notion of possible ways of causing it, becomes essential if it is to be carried on in a principled manner. This immediately raises the issues of content, objectives, and methods, concerns which Hirst has explored in more detail than anyone else. One of the defects of this discussion, from the point of view of language teachers, is its constant emphasis on substantive content. However, since it is the most sophisticated discussion available, it is necessary for us to consider the extent to which it can be related to language-teaching concerns. Having argued for the necessity of a planned curriculum, Hirst distinguishes between content and methods.

But if a curriculum is a plan of activities aimed at achieving objectives, it is a plan involving two other elements, a content to be used and methods to be employed to bring about learning. By content is usually meant the particular plays of Shakespeare that are studied, the particular elements of history considered – say, the foreign policy of Great Britain in 1914 – the particular social or moral problems that are discussed, and the like. And by methods, we usually mean the types of activities pursued by teachers and pupils together in discussions, group work, surveys, demonstrations, film and TV viewing, and so on.

(Hirst, 1974: 3)

Two points might be made in comment here. The first is that 'content' as Hirst defines it raises problems even in terms of his own arguments, for the content will have a varying relationship to the objectives of teaching, depending on why it has been chosen. Content in practice gives a context for the development of certain abilities, but – except when we view learning as simply the accumulation of 'facts' – other content could provide a context just as well, or if it could not, then the criteria for its selection become much more important than they appear in Hirst's argument. Hirst does in fact lead himself into an implicit recognition of this position in another paper when he argues that 'learning a concept is like learning to play tennis, not like learning to state the rules and principles that govern play' (Hirst, 1974: 125). This point will be further developed later. The other point is the apparent limitation of methods to 'types of activities', or what in language teaching have come to be called 'techniques' (Anthony, 1963). Doubts about these two categories are reinforced by Hirst's later remark (p. 5): 'Maybe many of the teaching methods used are excellent, but if the statement of content is taken as setting out what is to be learnt, there is a strong temptation to assume that traditional chalk and talk is pretty well all that is needed.'

In subsequent discussion Hirst's position is refined somewhat, and it turns out that he is more concerned with underlying concepts than with surface facts in spite of the identification of 'content' with 'what is to be learnt'. This leads him to ask the important question 'how are syllabuses and methods determined by the characteristics of what is to be taught and how are they to be determined by our empirical knowledge of teaching methods?' (p. 116). The paper ('The logical and psychological aspects of teaching a subject') does not answer that question, but it does explore problems in determining the characteristics of what is to be taught, though again with an emphasis on content subjects. The process of learning is complicated, but in order to facilitate it, different forms of thought must be distinguished, and this can only be done 'by reference to the particular set of terms and relations, which each of the distinct forms of thought employs' (p. 118). These forms of thought need to be taught by means of a logical sequence, but it is not necessary to claim that there is only one logical sequence for each subject. Examples of different forms of thought are science and history.

Now, what is interesting about this discussion is its emphasis on operational abilities, for there seems here to be a parallel with language learning which is worth pursuing. If even 'content' subjects are to be seen as providing a basis for developing certain kinds of conceptual relations, certain ways of seeing the world, and operating with categories derived from these perceptions, then the process of acquisition of a new culture appears similar to that demanded of language learners. Hirst does indeed relate this issue to language in school, and this point will be taken up again in the final section of this chapter.

One further clarification of the issues may be taken from Hirst's work before we turn to language teaching specifically. In an influential paper, he has analysed three concepts much referred to in educational literature as possible objectives in education: 'growth', 'needs', and 'interests' ('The nature and structure of curriculum objectives', Hirst, 1974: 16–29). All three of these he finds lacking as specifications of objectives on the grounds that all three obscure rather than clarify the nature of objectives. If we do not specify a direction for 'growth', we risk claiming that developing skills in burglary is a legitimate objective; 'saying what children need is only a cloaked way of saying what we judge they ought to have' (p. 17); and, similarly, interests can and will be socially moulded or created, so we should admit that we have a controlling influence over these too. Such discussion has relevance to recent work on language syllabuses.[6]

Teaching, then, may be seen as an attempt to cause changes in behaviour which result from changes in conceptualisation. The process of teaching, therefore, can be planned and discussed, while the activity itself can of course be observed. Thus it will be possible for us to engage in philosophical discussion relating to the nature of a particular teaching programme, and to use descriptive categories in an attempt to classify, and perhaps explain retrospectively, the behaviour of teachers and pupils in direct, or indirect, interaction. Thus far, the approaches both of philosophers like Hirst and of social scientists like Easton may have a role to play. But it is important to note that Hirst's work is, in an important sense, *preliminary* to teaching, and a social scientist's approach is *subsequent* to teaching. Neither of them can make predictions about the teaching process itself in terms of particular classes and particular teachers. Even if the social sciences are able to make probability statements, no class, let alone any individual student or teacher, is going to provide a large enough population for us to be able to say that *this* particular group is going to behave in a particular way. In terms of the four points with which we concluded our first section, then, we may observe:

16

1 that empirical evidence can, in principle, be available to inform our experience and intuitions about teaching;
2 that teachers do perceive that there are problems to be solved, though
3 such problems will need careful logical discussion in order to arrive at testable solutions;
4 but we have not yet established whether or not serious public testing of proposed solutions is possible in relation to teaching methodology, though the predictive power of observations based on the social sciences has been doubted.

This final, crucial question will be discussed in relation to the specific problems in language teaching.

1.3 Educational research and language-teaching methodology

If we conceive of methodological study as being the investigation of the total process of language teaching and learning in relation to existing institutions and practices, then we shall be forced to look upon it as an interdisciplinary study. In addition, for reasons which have been clarified by our examination of problems with traditional behaviourist models, we cannot reasonably ignore the complex situations in which people teach and learn. Perhaps it may help to clarify this point, with reference to the specific issue, by considering the major reason for a lack of transfer between one situation and others.

In a typical classroom there is likely to be at least one teacher and somewhere in excess, in normal school systems, of thirty students. Even without attempting to specify the subtle and indefinable relationship between language use and personal experience and context, there are still obviously a vast number of variables to respond to if we are to make valid predictions. Here is a crude attempt at classification of types of variable:

1 At the most general level the situation will be constrained by *national variables*. These will directly affect the teaching–learning situation and will be major indirect influences on the personal characteristics of both teachers and pupils. The major factors relevant to language teaching will be:
  a) national educational aims (in general)
  b) national educational aims for language teaching
  c) the nature of the social situation which causes particular languages to be taught.

  It should be noted that it is perfectly possible for (a), (b), and (c) all to conflict with one another.

2 These general factors will significantly affect *local situational variables*.
These will be affected
  a) through official policy decisions, or lack of decision, in relation to
      i)   size of class
      ii)   degree of compulsion exercised over pupils' choice of subject
      iii) quantity and intensity of instruction allowed
      iv)   amount of administrative support offered to the teacher (in the
            form of syllabuses, booklists, etc.)
      v)   physical resources available, both general (classroom space,
            desks, etc.) and pedagogical (visual aids, textbooks, etc.);
  b) through the unofficial climate of opinion in relation to
      vi)   control, class relationships and discipline
      vii) degree of interference tolerated (classes suddenly cancelled,
            electric drilling allowed in classrooms during lessons, etc.)
      viii) freedom of manoeuvre allowed to the teacher (the extent to which
            textbooks and official syllabuses can be criticised and changed,
            etc.).

3 *Pupil variables*, including:
  a) aptitude for language
  b) attitudinal factors
  c) motivation
  d) age
  e) nature of previous experience of learning, and of language learning.

All these will combine with other factors to form the individual pupil's
standard, and the combination and interaction of individual standards will
form the class standard.

4 *Teacher variables*, including:
  a) aptitude
  b) attitude
  c) motivation
  d) age
  e) previous experience
  f) training.

All of these will be in relation to language, and to teaching.

[*Variables in language teaching*   (adapted from Brumfit, 1980: 130–2)]

It should be noted that none of these factors yet takes into account the
specific choices of methodology, resources, and techniques that teachers
make; nor do they specify the delicate interactional factors which will
result from a teacher's past experience of individual pupils, or the knowledge of each other's background which participants in any interaction
must bring to bear on it.

A claim that we can predict closely what will happen in a situation as complex as this can only be based on either a view that human beings are more mechanical in their learning responses than any recent discussion would allow, or the notion that we can measure and predict the quantities and qualities of all these factors. Neither of these seems to be a sensible point of view to take.

But this does not mean that we cannot usefully talk about methodology at all; it simply entitles us to view with suspicion claims about the measurement of teaching effectiveness and overall generalisations about teaching processes, regardless of cultural and individual context. There seem to be two different basic reasons for our inability to transfer observations from one context to another. One is the sensitivity and fluid nature of the situation. The whole process of personal interaction is one of constant adjustment and readjustment by all parties to the interaction. Although we cannot make precise predictions here, we can certainly inform participants in interactions of the results of previous observations, whether these are formal observations or intuitions which result from experience. The other difficulty in transfer results from our dealing with value judgements all the time. Acts of teaching are not simply *directed* acts, they are *motivated* acts, in which the ethical goals of participants play a part. And the complexity of ethical choice is at least as great as the complexity of describing social interaction. We come back in part to Hirst's distinction between content and method, except that 'content' now has to be related to our choice of objectives, both long-term and short-term, and 'methods' has to be related to the kinds of interaction we choose. In both cases there is an inevitable process of improvisation, because decisions in each case depend on a constant reassessment of student reactions. Either way, there is an important role to be played by interpretations and assessments of experiences in other, similar situations. Such interpretations and assessments are the proper activities of methodologists. But the experiences in other situations can only inform, they cannot provide predictions.

In practice this means that the role of the methodologist is to describe and explore the range of possible options available to teachers in as principled a way as possible. This may involve such activities as assessment of theory and research relating to the subject being studied – in this case language – for its relevance to teaching; consideration of research in education, or in any of the disciplines which have a direct or indirect relationship to education, such as sociology or psychology or political science; or discussion of any philosophical issues which emerge from general educational debate. The main point is that, as with scientific work, the origin of the idea is unimportant – it may come from fiction, or anecdote – so long as it can be argued convincingly as a source of ideas for teachers. Where it will differ from scientific work is in the validation process. No one is going to prove, even provisionally, that a particular language-teaching procedure is better than another. Indeed, the major attempts to look globally at language-teaching methods have been shown to be deficient in a number of ways (Keating, 1963; Scherer and Wertheimer, 1964; P.D. Smith, 1970, for example, discussed by, among others, Freedman, 1971).[7] But as long as a constant process of discussion and feedback is maintained between the teaching profession in the classroom and those who write for and about it, the Popperian conditions will be met at a level appropriate to the problems being examined. Whether a more detailed and specific account of classroom activity will ever be possible remains, like all other questions, an open one.

But methodologists must continue to worry about their problems as best they can given the present state of our knowledge. They will perform no service to the profession if they imply a false rigour, in which scientific procedures are used to falsify claims where both the data and the falsification are dependent on procedures far from genuine classrooms. However, if the administrative means for feedback are created, encouraged and preserved, appropriate falsification will emerge at the level of generality at which statements can appropriately be made. That is to say that ranges of possible options will be proposed and explored. Teachers, on the basis of their experience and understanding of classrooms, will take up what looks possible, or what appears to answer the problems that are most immediately worrying. They will try it out, and accept or reject it in the context for which it is intended. A strong sense of an activist profession will create the conditions for such public 'falsification' of new and revised ideas, but such a sense needs to be created and fostered by the structure of teacher education, professional associations and professional advancement within a particular educational system. Nonetheless, the basis for such discussion exists. Methodology thus becomes a form of discussion analogous to the formation of political and social policy, rather than to the procedures of the descriptive sciences. The need for sensitive feedback and monitoring thus becomes crucial at all levels, within the classroom and without, but the search for easy answers has to be seen as inappropriate, just as it is inappropriate in determining broad social policies.

In language teaching there have been a number of different responses to doubts about methodology as science, as expressed above. It is probably not unfair to claim that many of them represent little more than an instinctive and unthought-out reaction. More serious have been attempts, such as Widdowson (1980) to link the procedures of science and literature by pointing out the role of metaphor, or of images of the world, as bases for scientific enquiry, functioning in a way similar to those of novels or other works of art. An alternative approach has been to relate foreign-language methodology explicitly to the social sciences, or at least to their descriptive apparatus. Strauss (1982), for example, regards foreign-language methodology as a 'special branch of the social sciences' (p. 2), but the attempt to define it within such a framework simply results in a specification of the interests of foreign-language methodologists, related in an *ad hoc* way to linguistic, psychological, philosophical and pedagogical issues. 'General laws' (the examples given are 'progression' and 'regression') are translated into 'principles', which in turn will be realised as 'methods', 'rules', 'techniques', 'exercises' and 'aids'. In fact, there seems to be some confusion of levels (p. 5), for at one point 'methods' and 'rules' are equated, at another everything is subsumed under 'methods', while they are still all treated as realisations of 'principles'. Nonetheless, it is useful to accept his relation between principles and methods; and the definition given, together with the reminder about the source of influence on the classroom, is important for the argument of this chapter.

Methods are considered to be intellectually formed prescriptions of future actions and as real forms of moving the subject-matter of fltl [foreign-language teaching and learning] alike. Principles alone cannot alter the substance in fltl, only methods can. This is achieved by means of techniques, rules, exercises, and objective means (= teaching aids).
(Strauss, 1982: 5)

However, for all the pretension, this seems to be no more than a rephrasing of Anthony's (1963) distinction between approach, method and technique. It is unclear that there has been any explicit gain from the alleged relationship with social sciences.

More valuable, perhaps, would be an attempt to link language pedagogy to the general development which schools try to promote. It has already been indicated that Hirst sees the development of concepts as closely allied to the 'symbols of our common languages' (Hirst, 1974: 83). He appears, in fact, to be arguing that the development must be closely tied to what is effectively the playing of language games: that is, operating with conventional rules of language which vary according to the appropriate mode of discourse. If this point of view is accepted – and acceptance or not must depend on the discussion of the nature of language which we shall address in the next chapter – we seem to have a possible means of linking language work to general pedagogy. If such links can be developed, they will have major implications for the status of language teaching.

We have seen, then, that it makes little sense to treat language teaching, or indeed any teaching, as if it can be prescribed as a result of experimentation or predictive hypothesising at a specific level. Nonetheless, it is possible to operate institutionally within a Popperian model of public accountability and feedback. As with any attempt to intervene in human action, the procedure must be more than simply a technology, for the process of understanding cannot be separated from the process of continuous intervention. The object of study is the adaptive power of teachers and learners – a power which can be both efficient and inefficient – and the process of adaptation can only be observed in interaction with the forces which try to direct adaptation. Methodology is the understanding and the appropriate guidance of these adaptive powers in relation to educational objectives. This chapter has also considered some examples of ways in which language teaching has been related to other disciplines, and the possibility of relating it to general conceptual development has been seen to have considerable potential.

2 Language and language acquisition: a contemporary view

I have argued in Chapter 1 that methodology in teaching is an attempt both to understand and to intervene in the process of language learning. Although the argument developed there may be applicable to the methodology of teaching any subject, we are concerned particularly with its implications for work with language, and consequently we need to examine the nature of language and language acquisition. In later chapters we shall explore some of the problems of relating linguistic and psychological ideas to the *practice* of language teaching, but in this chapter a basic statement will be presented of the contemporary consensus in these fields. For the purposes of my argument, it is not necessary for this statement to be too detailed, for I am concerned with the kind of overall picture of language available to teachers, not with specific evaluation of the various competing theories within linguistics or psycholinguistics. Thus I shall present a fairly succinct account of current views, though not one which is intended to be contentious. In fact, the general trend of contemporary work has, as we shall see, enabled commentators to present a much more socially sensitive view of language than was possible even fifteen years ago, and this has some significance for the attitude that I shall take to teaching procedures and syllabuses.

I shall start, then, by specifying recent ideas on the nature of language as a human phenomenon, and then consider successively the related processes of language acquisition and second-language acquisition.

2.1 The nature of human language

The kind of consensus on language which is normally available to teachers may be typified by a book such as Lyons' *Language and Linguistics* (1981). In this book, he quotes and criticises a number of twentieth-century definitions of language. Only Chomsky's, of the definitions given, does not view language primarily as a conventional symbol system concerned with communication or co-operation between people, and Lyons himself sees language as one among a number of other semiotic systems (Lyons, 1981: 3–11). This emphasis follows the lead of Saussure (1916: 33) in a concern to see language in the context of other communication frameworks.

Chomsky, however, produces a much more formal definition: 'From now on I will consider a language to be a set (finite or infinite) of sentences, each finite in length and constructed out of a finite set of elements' (Chomsky, 1957: 13). This is clearly a definition in terms of structure rather than function, and need not conflict with functional definitions – indeed, most linguists, insofar as they idealise their data, act as if this definition is valid, whether or not they are explicit about it. But the relationship between structure and function, if any, is a central issue in contemporary linguistics, and the interest has grown partly out of the way in which Chomsky has related the linguist's process of idealisation to actually occurring acts of language. 'We thus make a fundamental distinction between *competence* (the speaker-hearer's knowledge of his language) and *performance* (the actual use of language in concrete situations),' he writes (Chomsky, 1965: 4). The problem is that, while 'competence' has been specified with some precision, 'performance' seems to include not merely the lapses in performance which occur when knowledge is interfered with by fatigue or inattention, but also stylistic variation (Chomsky, 1965: 27) and acceptability (Chomsky, 1965, 10–15). Performance thus seems to embrace both the failure to achieve competence which is found in the traditional psychological distinction between what is known and what is actually done, and also certain other kinds of knowledge which allow us to produce utterances which are appropriate as well as grammatical.

There have been three main responses to this distinction. One has been to accept it as a useful basis for the consideration of the grammar of the language which must necessarily be idealised, and to concentrate on studies of competence, for reasons outlined in Lyons 1972: 56–61. This has been the tradition of transformationally orientated linguistics. A second has been to deny the usefulness of the concepts or the distinction. This has been Halliday's minority position:

Such a dichotomy runs the risk of being either unnecessary or misleading: unnecessary if it is just another name for the distinction between what we have been able to describe in the grammar and what we have not, and misleading in any other interpretation. The study of language in relation to the situations in which it is used . . . is a theoretical pursuit, no less interesting and central to linguistics than psycholinguistic investigations relating the structure of language to the structure of the human brain.[1]

(Halliday, 1970: 145)

As we shall see, this view has been influential in language teaching, but it has probably been less influential than that of the third position, which accepts a competence/performance distinction, but extends the notion of competence to embrace all rule-systems which describe our knowledge of language and how to operate with it. This view has led to the concept of communicative competence, discussed by a range of scholars including

Jakobovits (1970), Habermas (1970), Hymes (1971), and Savignon (1972), and implied earlier by Wales and Marshall (1966) and R.L. Cooper (1968) among others.[2] The literature on communicative competence has been surveyed by various writers with varying emphases (Le Page, 1975; Munby, 1978, chap. 1; Canale and Swain, 1980), but there is general agreement among applied linguists that it is necessary to specify as clearly as possible not only the formal features of linguistic systems but the ways in which these formal features may legitimately be operated. How this should be done will depend on the purpose for which a description is being devised. For language teachers there have been attempts to define the dimensions of language use from a number of different directions. These attempts, based on various language-related disciplines, serve to emphasize the complexity of language behaviour, though the extent to which an awareness of such complexity should affect language teaching remains a contentious issue. It must be recognised, of course, that attempts to explore the nature of language use, originating as they do in the preoccupations of different disciplines and traditions, cannot necessarily be expected to fit together as component parts in a single coherent theory of language. Nonetheless, the similarity of concern of the past decade or so cannot fail to produce results that are suggestive for applied linguists.

There are three important strands from the social sciences which have clarified our understanding of language: from anthropology, sociolinguistics and social psychology. Throughout the 1960s, Hymes (1964, 1967, 1968, 1971) explored ways in which utterances may be defined as appropriate to specific social contexts. The components of particular 'speech events' (1967) are analysed to show how such factors as participants, setting, scene, form of message, topic, purpose, and choice of code interact with one another. This ethnographic approach leads to a consideration of communicative competence, in direct and deliberate opposition to Chomsky's linguistic competence, in which the crucial questions are the extent to which something is formally possible, feasible, appropriate, and actually performed (Hymes, 1971: 18–19). Communicative competence, thus formulated, will include formal competence, but will extend that to embrace knowledge of the 'rules of use without which the rules of grammar would be useless' (Hymes, 1971: 15). This formulation enables Hymes to address questions which are obscured by the insistence of formal linguistics on idealisation, for while a grammar is socially neutral, competence in rules of use reflects ability to interact with social environment, and a possibility of differential competence emerges. However, the extent to which such rules of use are formalisable is a matter of debate; indeed, there is little agreement on what form such rules could take. What Hymes has done conveniently, though, is to provide a broad framework, even if often no more than metaphorical, for subsequent discussion of language as a system which is *performed* as well as known. At the same time, however, we are dependent on other areas of social science for empirical observations of what people actually do when they perform with language, and Hymes' categories provide a useful descriptive framework, even though they are not intended to provide a basis for generative rules.

One possible way of investigating what people actually do is to look at the language variations, formally measured, that occur in contextualised speech. Labov, particularly, has examined relations between sociolinguistic and formal patterns of language in order to produce rules based on probability (Labov, 1972). Other researchers (for example, Trudgill, 1974) have produced similar findings, but their direct value to language teaching will be limited unless convincing motivation can be found for the kinds of variation observed. Questions of this kind have been addressed by social psychologists, from a number of standpoints. Berger (1979), for example, has considered ways in which language strategies are used to develop mutual understanding. Bourhis, Giles, Leyens and Tajfel (1979) have shown how in Belgium, a Flemish speaker would more readily adopt Flemish (rather than French or English) in response to a Francophone speaker using the neutral language English when the speaker was perceived as threatening. And again, Bourhis and Giles (1977) have shown how in similar circumstances between Welsh and English speakers the Welsh accent is intensified. Day (1982) has shown how language attitudes and perceptions develop early, so that speakers from majority and minority groups already have strong in- and out-group perceptions, on the basis of language, by the age of three. Thus, perceptions of linguistic distinctions, and the manipulation of such distinctions for communicative or non-communicative purposes are factors to be taken into account both in language acquisition and language use. Such detailed examination of the role of language can also be interpreted within the broader and more speculative frameworks of Goffman (1959, 1961, 1967), in which strategies for human interaction are related to the nature of self-presentation and self-protection.

Further consideration of the implications of language in use has emerged from various traditions in philosophy. Most influential have been, on the one hand, speech-act theory, deriving from Austin (1962) via Searle (1969), and the co-operative principle of Grice (1975). This is not the place for a detailed description of the value of these principles for language teaching (see Schmidt and Richards, 1980), but it is important to note that Searle conceives of language as a series of acts in the world rather than as a collection of sentences, as TG appears to. This is a point which has been taken up extensively by Widdowson (1978a) in relation to language teaching. The Gricean co-operative principle provides, through a series of maxims (be as informative as required, truthful, relevant, brief and orderly – Grice, 1975: 45 ff.), a list of presuppositions about the nature of conversation which will enable participants to make sense of one another's contributions – at least for discussion and argument. Attempts to codify the ways in which we make sense have fed into ethnomethodological approaches to language, and into more formal attempts to describe the features of discourse. Thus there have been attempts to analyse telephone conversations (Schegloff, 1968), story telling (Sacks, 1972), the turn taking (Sacks, Schegloff and Jefferson, 1974), to give three typical examples, while all these approaches have contributed to the attempts of Birmingham linguists to structure spoken discourse in terms of hierarchical categories (Sinclair and Coulthard, 1975; Coulthard, 1977).

None of these approaches claims to link syntactic structure with the kinds of choices made by speakers, and of course, if such a link could be shown to be systematic, then the constraints of context and personal interaction would be linked with form in a genuine theory of performance. As indicated earlier, this is the major interest of Halliday (1973, 1978). Reversing the procedures of ethnomethodologists, he conceives of language as 'meaning potential' and attempts to relate this systematically to, on the one hand, the potential modes of behaviour available to a participant in a social situation, and, on the other, the available options in the formal linguistic systems. Even though many of the illustrations used may work only within a limited and fairly predictable field of operation (as in the punishment example (1973: 85–9), in which syntactic choices are related to the options available to a mother who disapproves of a child's action), nonetheless this is one of the few approaches to the study of linguistic system which conceives of meaning as a form of social action, and relates form specifically to the context of situation. Not surprisingly, then, it has been influential in discussions of communicative teaching.

The purpose of the preceding discussion has been to illustrate the way in which scholars in many disciplines have attempted to show the vast range of subtle variations which can in principle be exploited by language users. What they show cumulatively is that language cannot be thought of solely as a system of formal elements without taking away its major functions. A description of language which is independent of its function is unlikely to have much value to teachers and students who are concerned with developing a capacity to exploit the functional possibilities of a language. Is it possible, then, to give a brief account of language which recognises the role of language possessors as not only owners but also *users* of language? To do this it is necessary to recognise what may not have been apparent from the discussion so far, that language is a dynamic, not a static system.

The research so far considered has mainly been concerned with the various conventions that have arisen in the use of language, or particular languages, and with the ways in which these conventions are adjusted to varying situations. However, all these studies are necessarily based on some measure of idealisation, for while there may be some basic rules of interaction which will be universal (for example, two speakers operating loudly and simultaneously will have difficulty in establishing communication), the symbols used will almost always have an arbitrary relationship with what they refer to. This relationship will be negotiable within each speech community to such an extent that speakers of the same language often (but automatically, so that they are rarely aware of it) have to establish the extent of common meaning in the linguistic tokens with which they operate. This becomes obvious whenever there are dialect differences, but it is equally significant whenever there are misunderstandings between speakers of the same dialect who know each other well. All generalisations are based on a range of differing idiolects, and all idiolects are in principle infinitely malleable to the demands of an infinite number of situations and interlocutors. But we as language users have some influence over the extent to which we wish to be malleable. Stubborn people may choose to be more resistant than accommodating people – and groups of people may give greater or lesser social approval or support to stubbornness. Consequently, any model of language that we adopt for teaching must recognise that learners need to develop a capacity to operate with the target language sufficiently flexibly to be able to express themselves as much or as little as they wish to, and sufficiently firmly within an appropriate conventional model to be genuinely communicative. As Widdowson has described (1982), language rests on a permanent tension between co-operation, with its attendant risks, and security, with its attendant lack of communication.

The basic point is that within any language the range of possible interpretations of specific items is potentially infinite, although we have conventional expectations. Consider the following examples from English:

a)   Hand me my clubs.
b)   He clubbed my hand.
c)   Clubs dominate my hand.

Any user of English will be able to place some interpretation, with greater or lesser confidence, on each of these sentences, by creating a context – or in Widdowson's terms, converting them into utterances (Widdowson, 1979: 232–3). Native speakers, and those non-native speakers who have extensive experience of native-speaking environments, will possess intuitions about the likelihood of these sentences occurring, and about the range of possible settings through which they could be converted to utterances. Insofar as there are cultural stereotypes available, such intuitions will converge, so that many people would associate (a) with golf, all other factors being equal, (b) with a somewhat unusual and not strongly marked situation, perhaps children playing, and (c) with a card game. But none of these is absolute; indeed, as a non-card-player I am not entirely sure of the appropriateness of (c), and have therefore had to depend on information from those who do play cards – that is, speakers of that register of English. Now, while semantically there are clear and traceable relationships in etymology between the three examples of each of the two lexical items, 'club' and 'hand' used in these sentences, the exact way in which extension of meaning, through transfer of word class, metaphor, or conventional representation, has developed can only be understood through awareness of relationships in the world independent of language.

In principle, there is no limit to the possible range of extensions, associations and therefore meanings that may develop for any lexical item, because, as human beings, we possess the capacity to form associative ties between concepts, and to persuade each other of the value of such associations, so that they become conventionalised for particular groups.[3] Since the range of possible attributions for any referent, and therefore for any sign, are infinite, we shall never be able to specify the future development of meaning. We depend, therefore, as language users, on our ability to respond to the new conventions which confront us whenever we meet new groups of people, but the conventions will never be solely linguistic ones, for probability associations will have to derive from our expectations of what is being talked or written about as well as our anticipation of syntactic, phonological, or lexical items within the linguistic system itself.[4] The kinds of expectations that have been observed or hypothesised by the various kinds of research reported earlier in this section enable us to appreciate the complexity of the interacting systems of expectation that we operate. They also suggest, however, that we shall never, in principle, be able to specify what it is to know a particular language except in terms of general capacities to enter into negotiation with users of that language. The 'knowledge', whether of grammar, word meanings, functional conventions, or of cultural expectations, must be seen as merely a pedagogic device, a means of keeping the choppy water of social interaction calm enough for the neophyte to be able to practise in an environment which is untypically secure.

The model of language that is being proposed here, then, sees language use as a process of approximating the public avowals we make of our perceptions to other people's public avowals, to the extent necessary for us to perform effectively whatever it is we want to do with other people, or to obtain whatever it is we want to obtain from other people. It is by definition a process of compromise, insofar as it is socially aimed, but since each person has different needs and perceptions, each new engagement involves a newly negotiated compromise, though of course there are established routines wherever it will be more efficient – because we can predict that some needs and negotiations will recur – to assume that the common interest is understood by all participants. Thus negotiations of meaning between strangers may be protracted, while they establish the extent of their agreement about the purpose of the interaction (is it to ask the way, to get change for the telephone, to beg?) and about the amount of shared knowledge required for the interaction to be satisfactorily completed.[5] In situations where strangers customarily meet, such as lecture halls, formal interviews, or churches, the social and linguistic conventions will often be highly stylised so that contact can be made according to conventions that are already known, and negotiation of meaning can be limited to certain prearranged areas. The process of language use consists of a simultaneous response to a whole range of semiotic systems which are directly signalled (the language, the layout of a book, the appearance, gestures, proxemics of our interlocuters) together with a simultaneous response to a whole range of semiotic systems which are being referred to, directly or indirectly, in the message (see the sociological approach of Berger and Luckman, 1966, and work on symbolic interactionism, discussed by Argyle, Furnham and Graham, 1981: 16–18). Thus, if we listen to a lecture on literature, quite apart from the manifest codes of overt signs, we shall also have to respond to our awareness of lectures and speeches as events in education or outside it, of literature as a phenomenon, of the particular genres, authors, books being discussed, and to any specific connections made by the speaker which we have not already anticipated. The more familiar we are with the conventions of any of these, the greater our ability to recognise departures from the norm by the speaker in order to make new points. The less familiar we are, the harder we shall find it to recognise deviation and thus innovation. Conventions of this kind will not be possessed exclusively by particular languages. Some, such as those of United Nations debates, will be deliberately created across linguistic boundaries; many, such as those of physics or literary criticism, will spread gradually but not necessarily intentionally wherever there is international interest; others will remain local or sectarian. In all cases, though, the conventions will develop to establish ease of communication, and will result from the wish to communicate and co-operate. Learning to use language is learning to converge (for communication) without loss of identity (for our identity is found in the differences on which the need to communicate is based).

2.2 Language acquisition

If we accept the view of language outlined above, we should expect to see an interest in the process of interaction among psycholinguists, and indeed this is a clearly observable phenomenon of the last few years. From the concern with the child's syntactic development, influenced by struc-

tural linguistics (R. Brown, 1973), and the concern with cognitive development in the post-transformational period (Moore, 1973; Macnamara,
1977), there has been a steady move towards an interest in pragmatics
and the acquisition of discourse. In Britain, a seminal work in this area has
been Halliday's (1975) study of his own child. Halliday, as we have seen,
is concerned with the meaning potential of language. His initial procedure
is worth quoting:

In the first place, there are the observations relating to the use of language by a
very small child. In the second place, there are the theoretical considerations
about linguistic functions; and these theories include, in turn, first those which
are essentially linguistic in nature, functional theories of language and of the
semantic system, and secondly those which are essentially extra-linguistic in
nature, sociological theories embodying some concept of cultural transmission
and processes of socialization. Taking these factors into account I had suggested
a set of functions which would serve for the interpretation of the language of a
very young child; that is, as an initial hypothesis for some kind of functional or
sociolinguistic approach to early language development. The postulated set of
functions was as follows:
(1) Instrumental
(2) Regulatory
(3) Interactional
(4) Personal
(5) Heuristic
(6) Imaginative

(Halliday, 1975: 18–19)

Then, having defined these six more clearly,he adds, 'Later on there is in
fact a seventh to be added to this list; but the initial hypothesis was that
this seventh function, although it is the one which is undoubtedly dominant in the adult's use of language, and even more so in the adult's image
of what language is, is one which does not emerge in the life of the child
until considerably after the others. This is the one that we can call the
informative function of language . . . '. In the event, although the first six
functions appeared more or less together in two separate stages (the first
four and later the next two), the informative function was indeed last to
appear, at about twenty-one months, six months later than the last of the
others.

   Other researchers have charted the continuity between mother–child
interaction before speech has developed (Dore, 1974; Ringler *et al.* 1975),
the development of routines at the stage of what Halliday calls 'proto-
language' (Halliday, 1975: 25; Gleason and Weintraub, 1976), and the
development of more complex syntax in relation to external social stimuli
(Ingram, 1978). Wells (1981), in a comprehensive survey of the literature
which shows how the ability to converse arises steadily out of the total
interactive context of babyhood, proceeds to demonstrate in detail the
ways in which adults support and assist children's conversation by, for

example, checking and expanding their contributions (Wells, 1981: 101–9). The exact procedures used are not important for our argument, so long as we note the impossibility of isolating children's language experience at the early stages from the process of interaction. A consequence of this is that two aspects of the process of language development can be identified: one in which the child uses words within the framework of an already developed communicative ability – conventional words replace gestures or personal, idiosyncratic words; the other is the child's 'creative exploitation of the inherent function of words' (Lock, 1980: 194). Children try to make explicit what is implied by what they say, in order to establish which of the many possible relationships for any words and for what they refer to are the ones appropriate in a given context.

Lock relies heavily for this view on the work of Greenfield and Smith (1976), but similar conclusions can be drawn from Eve Clark's series of studies (collected in Clark, 1979). She summarises her position thus:

The first major hypothesis is that children acquire simpler words within a semantic field before they acquire words that are more complex. The second hypothesis is that the more children's non-linguistic strategies lead them to the 'right' meanings, the easier it should be to map ideas onto words. Their a priori knowledge, then, may say which words are easy, and hence acquired first. Semantic complexity and non-linguistic knowledge jointly play a major role in children's acquisition of word meanings.

(Clark, 1979: 7)

With minor adjustments, both these hypotheses are borne out by her investigations. As an illustration of how her work fits in with our view of language, and with Lock's comments above, let us consider the investigation of the acquisition of deixis (Clark and Sengul, 1978). The investigators conclude that, with reference to *here*, *there*, *this*, and *that*, children first learn that these terms are in fact deictic, and then acquire the two basic principles associated with these terms (their relationships to speaker and to distance) in three stages: first without making contrasts, then making partial contrasts, and finally making the full contrast. But just as important for our argument is the fact that, while all children tested went through these three stages, the strategies they used differed. The test used required them to move toys, and some children, at the early stages, showed a bias towards the toys nearest the speaker while others showed a bias to toys nearest themselves. The structure of the experiment, though, meant that some children's bias accidentally led them towards correct answers for *this* and not *that* and some the other way round. But this varied when the speaker changed position, and moved from opposite the child to beside it, and repeated the instruction. The experiment showed that each child was consistent, but that the strategies by which they moved towards acquisition of the full meaning varied according to their initial bias. This is a particularly important point to make, for it illustrates the way in which there will be variable interactive processes in the mastery of the language system as it relates to such factors as speaker position and relationship with listener.

For the purposes of our argument there would be little value in attempting to give a more comprehensive overview of the current state of language acquisition theory and research. The field is at the moment too diffuse, the amount of research too vast, and the theoretical presuppositions of researchers too varied for there to be a universally accepted paradigm. But we have seen that there is increasing interest in the interaction of socio-psychological processes and language development, and that this interest is compatible with the general view of the nature of language that was outlined at the end of the first section of this chapter. Halliday gives the clearest statement of the position:

> Meaning is at the same time both a component of social action and a symbolic representation of the structure of social action. The semiotic structure of the environment – the ongoing social activity, the roles and statuses, and the interactional channels – both determines the meanings exchanged and is created by and formed out of them. This is why we understand what is said, and are able to fill out the condensations and unpeel the layers of projection. It is also why the system is permeable, and the process of meaning subject to pressure from the social structure . . . The reality that the child constructs is that of his culture and sub-culture, and the ways in which he learns to mean and to build up registers – configurations of meanings associated with features of the social context – are also those of his culture and sub-culture.
>
> (Halliday, 1975: 143)

The important question for the rest of this chapter is the relevance of such a model to the acquisition and learning of a second language.

2.3 Second-language acquisition

Large numbers of people never acquire a second language to a high level of proficiency. This has had two interrelated consequences for work on second-language acquisition. First, it has led to the assumption that acquiring a second language is in some sense different from acquiring a first language, and second, it has led to the institutionalisation of second-language learning to a much greater extent than with first language. Clearly, there are two ways in which the acquisition of a second language must differ from that of a first language. First-language acquisition is in some sense the simultaneous development of the faculty of language as well as of the structure of a particular language, and it is apparently a natural and automatic product of the process of socialisation with adult human beings. However, although neither of these features may appear at first sight to be applicable to second-language development, we have to be careful not to be the prisoners of our own constructs. These differences may be inevitable in communities which are either so isolated or so centralised that the concept of 'mother tongue' is clear-cut and uncontentious, but for many communities the issue is much less straightforward (Bamgbose, 1976; Cummins, 1979). It is true that *initial* language learning is the simultaneous development of language and of particular language(s), but where children are brought up in bilingual or multilingual environments they will grow up bi- or multi-lingual as long as several languages are functionally necessary to them (De Houwer, 1982; Giles and Byrne, 1982), to such an extent that Swain was willing to title her doctorate thesis 'Bilingualism as a First Language' (Swain, 1972). Furthermore, when bilinguals are speaking together, the process of language shift seems to be exploited as naturally as, and for similar purposes to, dialect shift. It makes more sense to attribute lack of success in second-language acquisition to the issues of age and social context than to the demands of second languages in themselves. Swain makes this point clear:

... a child who hears nothing but English as he grows up is considered to have learnt English as a first language ... His English, however, will consist of a number of codes, for example a code he uses when speaking to babies, a code he uses when speaking with his peers, etc. ... The speech of a child who hears English and French as he grows up will also consist of several codes. Thus he should be considered to have learned French and English as a first language.

(Swain, 1972: 238–9)

But there is a sense also in which the adult continues to develop and modify the language acquired in early childhood. While the syntactic system usually remains relatively stable, phonology can be adjusted deliberately, and semantic relations may be subject to a great deal of change. Some of the ways in which these changes may be observed were described earlier in this chapter. For the purposes of our argument we need simply to note that if the linguistic system is indeed dynamic, and is indeed altered by speakers for their own purposes, then adults' manipulation of codes *within* and *across* language boundaries need not be considered as in principle different processes. (Note, for example, R.A. Hudson (1981: 336): 'There is no clear or qualitative difference between so-called "language-boundaries" and "dialect-boundaries".') However, when the adult learns a foreign language, the difference will lie in the extent to .which the tokens of the system have to be acquired independently of the perceptions of the semantic value of the system, for the adult will be far closer, through experience of meaning in the world via mother tongue and through the interest in the target culture that has led to the choice of the language to be studied, to the potential meanings of the target language than the child will be, at least at first, to the potential meanings of the culture into which the child is being socialised. The strategies that the older learner adopts could therefore be different from those adopted by very young children – but only in relation to these characteristics.

For second-language learners, as for native speakers, the process of acquisition will often be closely bound up with context, both at the level of the social group and individually. Giles and Byrne (1982: 35), after surveying the literature on intergroup relationships and language acquisition, propose that:

subordinate group members will most likely not achieve native-like proficiency in the dominant group's language when:
1 ingroup identification is strong and language is a salient dimension of ethnic group membership;
2 insecure inter-ethnic comparisons exist (e.g. awareness of cognitive alternatives to inferiority);
3 perceived ingroup vitality is high;
4 perceived ingroup boundaries are hard and closed;
5 weak identification exists with few other social categories, each of which provides inadequate group identities and an unsatisfactory intragroup status.

When the converse applies, they propose, native-like proficiency is more likely to be achieved.

Although these proposals have not yet been empirically verified as a package, they are consistent with the proposals of many researchers and empirical findings (for example, contributors to Giles, 1977). The relationship of second-language learning to group membership is significant for education as well as intergroup relations outside school, a point which will be taken up in Chapter 6.

In relation to individual learning, a number of commentators have emphasized the advantages of second-language learners operating in a social context similar to that encountered by mother-tongue learners (Ervin-Tripp, 1974; Hatch and Long, 1980). Others have investigated the process of negotiation of meaning (Schwartz, 1980) by second-language learners, and the use of language in context by children (Huang and Hatch, 1978) and adults (Allwright, 1980) as they learn. All these studies demonstrate language use similar to that observable by first-language learners and users. Furthermore, failure to learn may be attributed to an inability or unwillingness to interact (Schumann, 1976: 403). There is little doubt that learners will operate with second languages as they have in their mother tongues, whenever an opportunity is provided – unless there are strong ingroup reasons for resisting contact with the target language. However, most language teaching gives little opportunity for such activity.

At the same time, though, it is important to note that the process of second-language acquisition is complex at all ages. No simple before and after 'critical-period' model will be appropriate.[6] Hatch (1978: 12–18) notes the variation in the ease with which different young children acquired second languages, ranging from one six-year-old who appeared to acquire nothing from the first seven months of her immersion in English to others with extremely rapid development. Furthermore, frustrations and difficulties, as well as conscious attempts to learn, are reported, in ways similar to those attested to by adults (Pickett, 1978). Nor are children necessarily unaware of the linguistic process: the revised version of Leopold's bibliography of child language lists fifteen studies of children's metalinguistic awareness as they acquire language (Leopold, 1972). Hatch concludes (1978: 17) that recent studies of second-language acquisition 'show overall similarities in acquisition strategies whether the learner is child or adult'. But she also points out that 'the studies show considerable variation among learners at one age group and also across the age range'. McLaughlin (1978a: 208) points out some of the advantages that adults bring to bear on language-learning tasks. They can, for example, use more effective memorisation strategies so that they can retain input for longer; they have a greater experience of the resources of their first language, and can have recourse to the lexicon as a means of guessing items in the new language; they can process information more quickly; they have a much greater knowledge of the world. But he points out also that these advantages need not result in differences in kind between strategies: children too make use of these resources as far as they can, and there is enough evidence of similarities between adult and child second-language production to suggest that differences between these two groups are not fundamental. Between learners themselves, however, there may be variation in strategy, both in the classroom (Naiman, Fröhlich, Stern and Todesco, 1978: 100) and in natural settings with children (Lily Wong Fillmore, 1979).

We have seen, then, that the close connection between language and social relationships applies both to first- and second-language development, and that there need not be basic differences between adult and child learning. We may also add that the interaction between language development and psychosocial situation is likely to be a major area of study in the next decade, to judge by the number of recent papers calling for such a shift of emphasis (Tarone, 1979; McLaughlin, 1980; Canale and Swain, 1980, for example). But most intensive second-language learning takes place in classrooms, and it is worth considering the implications of the current research position for pedagogical acquisition. A number of commentators (for example, Jakobovits and Gordon, 1974, chap. 1; Sajavaara, 1980), have emphasized the undesirable effects of linguistic preoccupations on pedagogy. The preoccupation of pronunciation teachers with minimal-pair activities rather than with intonation and rhythm, or of audiolingual teaching procedures with phonology and syntax at the expense of meaning, are only two examples of teaching following the capacity of linguists to make satisfactory descriptions rather than the capacity of teachers to achieve successful learning. Sajavaara points out that the neglect of the lexicon may be a result of the autonomous status awarded to grammar by linguists. But the limited access of the learner to linguistic data, the ways in which educational institutions constrain interaction, and the instinctive processing procedures of normal learners will all mean that learners are in quite different positions from linguistic analysts. As Sajavaara says:

> production and reception are *creative* processes, and the establishment of communication between the two interactants is based only partially on rules which exist in the speech community and are available to its members through socialization and language acquisition. As important as such rules are various negotiation processes which are created *ad hoc* in each individual communicative situation. The linguist's description of the linguistic system functioning in such an interactive process cannot catch the creative aspect, the rules that are made by participants . . .
>
> (Sajavaara, 1980: 2)

Such a dichotomy in principle (emphasized within formal linguistics as that between language system and language behaviour: Lyons, 1977: 27–9) has led to a distinction which has been proposed for language learning and for pedagogy in a number of guises. The most fully developed and sophisticated version of the distinction is that expounded by Krashen (1976 and 1981a) as between 'learning' and 'acquisition'. He himself (Krashen, 1979) has drawn attention to three other versions of the same general distinction, and I propose to add two other versions, my own and Rivers', so that we have a table as follows:

1		2
mechanisms that guide 'automatic' performance	—	mechanisms that guide puzzle- or problem-solving performance (Lawler and Selinker, 1971)
skill-using	—	skill-getting (Rivers, 1972)
acquisition	—	learning (Krashen, 1976)
implicit knowledge	—	explicit knowledge (Bialystok and Fröhlich, 1977)
expression rules	—	reference rules (Widdowson, 1978b)
fluency	—	accuracy (Brumfit, 1979)[7]

[*Learning and acquisition-type distinctions*]

In this table, column 1 refers to the creation of meaning and is utterance-based, whereas column 2 refers to the creation of language forms, and is sentence-based. But to say this immediately reveals the defect of grouping all these dichotomies together, for some are primarily psychological in motivation and others pedagogical, some have wider relevance than language teaching and some are specific to that activity. Nonetheless, whether we are thinking of the description of the process or the activation of the process, it is important to note that a number of writers, working independently, have found it helpful to distinguish those mechanisms, largely cognitive, by which we understand the systems of language from those mechanisms, less described and perhaps less describable, by which we operate the systems naturally.

We have seen, then, that linguists, anthropologists, sociolinguists, psycholinguists, and sociologists are increasingly concerned with the operation of language in social relationships, and with the possible inter-action between linguistic form and social situation. A concern for such interaction has direct implications for a definition of the nature of language acquisition and probably for second-language development. What it implies for second-language work in classrooms is currently being debated, and will be discussed in detail in the next two chapters. But several commentators have found it necessary to posit alternative mechanisms or activities to allow for the formal learning element in foreign-language work, on the one hand, and the creative construction through meaningful interaction implied by current acquisition theories, on the other. In the next chapter, we shall take up the argument for making such distinctions, and later explore their implications for language teaching. We shall also examine the extent to which they will enable us to link pedagogy to the view of language and language acqui-sition that has been outlined in this chapter.

3 Language form and language value

3.1 An initial historical note

We have seen in Chapter 2 how linguistic variation is a direct consequence of the need to communicate in a variety of situations to various types of people. We have also seen how language acquisition is intimately related to the process of using language in varied contexts. In this chapter we shall be examining the extent to which the entries in column 1 of our table at the end of Chapter 2 fit in with this view of language acquisition, and also the extent to which there is a need to have entries under column 2, and the relationships between the two types of entry. Linguistic theory, as we have seen, has constantly been concerned with distinguishing what is systematisable within the language from what is (possibly) systematisable as the language is used in the world, and even Chomsky is happy, in recent papers, to discuss 'grammatical competence' in contrast to 'pragmatic competence' (Chomsky, 1980: 59, and 224–5). Discussions of word-meaning, whether in terms of denotation and connotation, or in relation to the medieval concerns with 'essence' and 'accidence' and with words as entries in a dictionary and as entries in an encyclopaedia, are concerned with a similar distinction between what is highly conventionalised and relatively un-negotiable and what is socially constructed and relatively easy to change in a principled way. We seem to have a three-cornered relationship between the learner as a language user and the language itself:

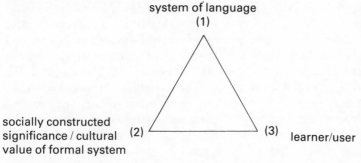

system of language
(1)

socially constructed
significance / cultural (2)
value of formal system

(3) learner/user

All three of these elements interact with one another, but arguments about teaching methodology may be seen as arguments about directionality: advocates of direct method and communicative approaches will tend to assume a clockwise process:

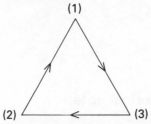

Those who believe in a conscious, strongly cognitive learning procedure will act as if the process operates in an anti-clockwise direction:

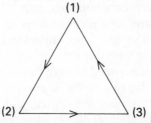

The 'formal system' (1) will include any idealised syntactic forms, diction-ary definitions, etc., while (2) will include all the values and associations which can only develop out of use and which will be liable to slight re-negotiation in each new environment.

This diagram links the need for the learner to acquire a system to the distinction between formal knowledge and practical ability to use. Both of these distinctions have been important in discussions of language learn-ing for a long time. The latter underlies Locke's remark, with reference to the learning of Latin, that 'If grammar is taught at any time, it must be to one who can speak the language already' (Locke, 1693: paragraph 168; Axtell, 1968: 269). The recognition of systematic relations between all elements, with implications for learning, is found in Humboldt: 'In order to enable man to understand only one single word . . . as an articulated sound that designates a concept, the whole of language in its structure must already lie in him. *There is nothing single in the language, every one of its elements announces itself only as part of a whole*' (Humboldt, 1903; quoted in Apel, 1976: 45; my italics). The recognition or acquisition of a *system* can only result from a *continuing* exposure to language, for it is not possible to be exposed to all elements of the system simultaneously.

De Quincey produces a distinction which is superficially similar to some of those made at the end of Chapter 2:

The *knowledge* of Greek must always hold some gross proportion to the time spent upon it – probably, therefore, to the age of the student; but the *command* over a language, the power of adapting it plastically to the expression of your own thoughts, is almost exclusively a gift of nature, and has very little connection with time.

(De Quincey, 1822: 48)

A little later comes a claim which is even closer:

Universally I contend that the faculty of clothing the thoughts in a Greek dress is a function of natural sensibility, in a great degree disconnected from the extent or accuracy of the writer's grammatical skill in Greek.

(De Quincey, 1822: 49)

While it is clear that De Quincey is not thinking here of language as inter-action so much as expression, the distinction is nonetheless between formal knowledge and effective use, and the emphasis on the relation between language and thought anticipates post-Vygotsky mother-tongue methodologists such as Dixon (1967) and Britton (1970).

For institutionalised language teaching, it is only with the discussions leading up to the Reform Movement of the nineteenth century that we begin to see some elements of the later dichotomy emerging, and even these are implicit rather than explicit. Claude Marcel (1853: cited from Howatt, 1984: 'Individual reformers', 153) advanced as Axiomatic Truth No. 8 that 'the mind should be impressed with the idea before it takes cog-nizance of the sign that represents it'. And Howatt comments, 'What Marcel is getting at here is something more complex than the general notion that comprehension precedes production. He means that the com-prehension of meaning precedes the acquisition of the linguistic elements used in its communication. We do not, strictly speaking, understand what people say, we understand what they mean.' (Howatt, 1984: 'Individual reformers', 153.) It is this view, presumably, which leads us to distinguish good communicators from good language learners. Margaret Mead insists on this distinction for herself, but the way in which she does so raises more questions about what we mean by language than she allows:

I am not a good mimic and I have worked now in many different cultures. I am a very poor speaker of any language, but I always know whose pig is dead, and, when I work in a native society, I know what people are talking about and I treat it seriously and I respect them, and this in itself establishes a great deal more rapport, very often, than the correct accent. I have worked with other field workers who were far, far better linguists than I, and the natives kept on saying they couldn't speak the language, although they said I could. Now, if you had a recording it would be proof positive I couldn't, but nobody knew it! You see, we don't need to teach people to speak like natives, you need to make the other people believe they can, so they can talk to them, and then they learn.

(Mead, 1964: 189; quoted in Crymes, 1980: 1)

Allwright (1977: 167–8) makes use of this distinction in asking, 'Are we teaching *language* (for communication)? *or* Are we teaching *communi-cation* (via language)?' and discusses the implications of accepting the latter for a minimal teaching strategy. All three of these writers maintain a distinction, though the classroom implications they might wish to present as a result of making the distinction will vary. For the moment, though, we shall leave this point to be taken up later. In spite of the various comments, suggesting or implying a linguistic/pragmatic split with potential relevance to language learning, the most important point to note is that in none of the historical surveys of language teaching that I have examined (Escher, 1928; Kelly, 1969; Howatt, 1984) does the kind of distinction we have been exploring receive any prominence. This may have been because advocates of various forms of more or less direct method, going back at least to Quintilian,[1] took such a distinction for granted, but it is certainly arguable that only in recent years have the contributions from sociology and social psychology enabled us to describe with any precision the complexities of fluent, natural language use.

3.2   The case for a polarity

Let us return to the six different polarities identified at the end of Chapter 2. Although each of them was devised in a different context, they share some features. Lawler and Selinker's distinction is part of an argument about the relationship between linguistics and language teaching. They are particularly concerned to clarify questions which might be important for language teaching whether or not they are important in linguistics. The distinction they make between automatic activity and problem-solving activity is concerned both with speed and processing. After discussing it in the terms used by Krashen, they rephrase the distinction for language teaching as:

1   performance in the second language in which the learner has time to consciously apply grammatical rules no matter how such rules are coded, and
2   performance in a second language in which automatic application of rules under conditions of speed and spontaneity is necessary.

(Lawler and Selinker, 1971: 38)[2]

It is clear that this formulation leads the way to Krashen's claim that there are two distinct processes at work, rather than a sequence, as assumed throughout audiolingual teaching, and in Rivers' formulation. Rivers is of course thinking about the teacher's point of view, and there are no necessary assumptions about the means of causing 'skill-getting' in distinguishing it from 'skill-using'. Nonetheless, by claiming that there are two identifiable stages in the teaching process, Rivers does suggest a complementary relationship, in which one feeds in to the other, which does not necessarily follow from Lawler and Selinker's position. The research enquiry that they demand could in principle lead to the abolition of a need for skill-getting activities – if, for example, it was found that two completely different rule-systems operated, and that one could not be transformed into the other. And, although he has been ambiguous on this issue in his more recent writings,[3] Krashen has often implied that the research in Second Language Acquisition in the 1970s shows a lack of contact between the two systems which would make nonsense of many claims of language teachers over the past two millennia. We shall consider his arguments in more detail later, but let us first place them in the context of the other dichotomies. Bialystok and Fröhlich (1977) distinguish between implicit and explicit knowledge, but since they refer to Krashen himself for this distinction we can conveniently treat it as the kind of knowledge that results from acquisition and learning respectively in his model, and discuss its implications while discussing that. Widdowson's distinction is between 'expression rules' (rules which govern what the learner does with language) and 'reference rules' (which characterise the learner's knowledge) (Widdowson, 1978b: 13).[4] However, this distinction is advanced with considerably more explanatory potential than the previous distinctions, for he does not consider these two sets as simply unsituated sources of language production.

What happens, I suggest, is that the learner is provided with a set of reference rules which he will act upon with a fair degree of success in those teaching situations which require simple conformity to them. The more he is required to use these rules for a communicative purpose, however, the more likely he is to adopt the normal communicative strategy of simplification; the more likely he is, in other words, to behave like a normal human being and develop expression rules to facilitate communication.

(Widdowson, 1978b: 15)

Expression rules, then, are the rules of normal communication, as applied by language learners to the language items they have so far been exposed to. Hence, with second-language learners as with young mother-tongue learners, they may well appear deviant from adult rule-systems or target rule-systems. Widdowson continues to consider various ways of teaching which would be more orientated to the development of adequate expression rules, but the suggestions – notional–functional syllabus design, teaching subject matter through the medium of the second language – are not explicit enough to deal with the problem of where reference rules come from for second-language learners to act upon. I shall discuss this point in relation to the accuracy/fluency distinction, but before that, it is important to note the dynamic potential of Widdowson's formulation in contrast to the others. Of the earlier distinctions, only that of Rivers implied any systematic relationship between the two sides, and that relationship could be realised through any learning theory. Widdowson, however, proposes an explanation for why the two systems may coexist in the same learner, and an account of the language-learning process which both allows for learner initiative and for the discrepancy between teaching and performance. It is also quite distinct in type from the Krashen-associated distinctions, for they are concerned with measurement of the linguistic system, while Widdowson is concerned with what is done in the process of interaction.

We have, then, two groups of distinctions so far. In one, a process of 'acquisition' may provide 'implicit knowledge' which is used through 'mechanisms that guide automatic performance', and this is contrasted with a process of 'learning' which may provide 'explicit knowledge' used through 'mechanisms that guide puzzle- or problem-solving performance'. While this is to oversimplify, it is certainly within the spirit of Krashen's grouping (1979). The implication for this group is that the latter may be irrelevant to the former, for if no principled relationship can be detected between them, there is no argument for using the latter when competence with a language is desired, for successful language use always appears to be automatic and based on implicit knowledge for most of the time.

The other two distinctions do specify a relationship between the two sides. Rivers, looking at the issue from the perspective of the teacher, simply codifies the assumptions underlying audiolingual practice (and, if we ignore the specific connotations of 'skill', of all language-teaching methods which assume presentation and practice strategies as a prerequisite of natural use) and sees them as successive stages in the learning, and therefore teaching, process. It would be possible to accept this formulation in terms of a range of learning theories, mentalist or behaviouralist, providing that a separation between performance and preparation for performance is accepted. The crucial question is the nature of the changes between the situation of use and the situation of preparation. The convention for language teaching has often been to separate out the component parts, but it is noteworthy that, in the standard work on skills, Welford (1968: 291) states that 'where the whole task is a closely co-ordinated activity . . . the evidence suggests that it is better to tackle the task as a whole' rather than learn one part at a time. He continues: 'Any attempt to divide it up tends to destroy the proper co-ordination of action and subordination of individual actions to the requirements of the whole . . . and this outweighs any advantage there might be in mastering different portions of the task separately.' Nonetheless, Rivers' distinction recognises the characteristic assumption of much pedagogy, and could be related satisfactorily to Widdowson's, for the activities conventionally regarded as 'skill-getting' can be seen as the establishment of 'reference rules' by learners, and 'skill-using' as the operation of 'expression rules'. Rivers, however, offers no more than a descriptive distinction, whereas Widdowson's is an explanatory hypothesis. Pedagogically, though, they both have merit over the other set, for they can be explicitly related to

teachers' traditional behaviour. This does not, of course, constitute a justification for these positions, but it does enable Widdowson's, in particular, to claim to be a possible explanation of teaching behaviour as well as
of the observed difficulties of learners transferring from formal to
informal language activities in the classroom.[5]

Krashen's position has been advanced with great persuasiveness and
massive documentation for the past decade, and has been the subject of
several careful and critical analyses (his major papers are collected in
Krashen, 1981a, and for criticisms see McLaughlin, 1978b; James, 1980;
Sharwood Smith, 1981; Bibeau, 1983). It is not necessary for this argument to review the whole context of Second Language Acquisition
studies, though one of the major areas of contention is the extent to which
morpheme studies justify the notion of invariant order of acquisition
(Larsen-Freeman, 1975; Rosansky, 1976; Andersen, 1977). It is the
other two main aspects which have been criticised that are directly relevant to pedagogy, for even if we accept the notion of invariant order we
still need to consider whether a complete lack of connection between
acquisition and learning can be argued for, and from that we shall need to
examine the implications of the distinction for the practice of language
teaching.

The distinction between explicit and implicit knowledge, on which the
learning/acquisition distinction has been based, poses major methodological problems, for implicit knowledge can only be inferred, whereas
explicit knowledge can be revealed by the knower. Krashen's monitor
model has an intuitive attractiveness, partly because of its simplicity, and
partly because it clearly describes a process that all self-conscious learners
will recognise.

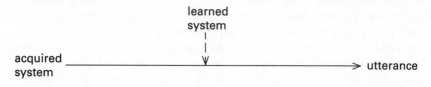

[*Monitor model*   (Krashen, 1981a: 2)]

To quote the introduction to Krashen's collected papers, and therefore
presumably a carefully considered statement:

The fundamental claim of Monitor Theory is that conscious learning is available
to the performer only as a *Monitor*. In general, utterances are initiated by the
acquired system – our fluency in production is based on what we have 'picked up'
through active communication. Our 'formal' knowledge of the second language,
our conscious learning, may be used to alter the output of the acquired system,

sometimes before and sometimes after the utterance is produced. We make these changes to improve accuracy, and the use of the Monitor often has this effect.
(Krashen, 1981a: 2)[6]

It is unlikely that anyone would wish to quarrel with the proposition that second-language learners, and sometimes native speakers, produce more or less automatic language, and sometimes monitor it more or less self-consciously, so that they alter it either as they produce it – if they have time – or by correction immediately afterwards. Such alterations may well be to 'improve accuracy', though it is unclear whether changes of that sort are to be regarded as different from similar changes and rephrasings to improve precision – for example, by selection of a different lexical item, or by any other adjustment or fine-tuning of the flow of speech. However, the claim that conscious learning is available *only* as a monitor is in principle unfalsifiable (as McLaughlin 1978b, and James, 1980, indicate), and anyway raises questions which create logical nonsense. As McLaughlin (1978b: 318) points out, the relationship between conscious learning and unconscious acquisition can only be supported by arguments based on 'subjective, introspective, and anecdotal evidence'. He suggests instead a distinction between 'controlled' and 'automatic' processing, since it 'enables one to avoid disputes about "conscious" or "subconscious" experience, since the controlled–automatic distinction is based on behavioral acts, not on inner states of consciousness'.

In his reply to this paper, Krashen claims simply to be using the usual procedures of psychology in postulating a hidden distinction (Krashen, 1979: 152), but he does not explain how the distinction is preferable to one based on more overt behaviour. What is more important, though, is the extent to which the two concepts can be regarded as totally independent of each other. Krashen equivocates a little (compare 'conscious learning is quite different from acquisition and *may be* a totally independent system' – Krashen, 1978: 22, my italics – with 'conscious learning *does not* initiate utterances or produce fluency' – ten lines later, my italics again); but the general argument clearly moves towards the view that learning does not contribute to acquisition and that natural language use arises out of acquisition, not out of learning.[7] This clearly has worried a number of experienced teachers. Stevick, for example, produces a modification of the monitor ('The Levertov Machine') which greatly complicates the model, but does enable it to reflect an interaction between acquisition and learning rather than two separate, even antagonistic, processes (Stevick, 1980: 267–82).[8]

Pressed this far, the distinction raises many difficulties. It requires us, for example, to distinguish between language instances that are constructed as a result of rules from those that crop up, either accidentally in other people's speech, or fluently (by acquisition) in our own, and to credit the two with different status as input. That is to say that a sentence that we know to be grammatical (perhaps because we have checked it consciously in a grammar book, and verified it in a text that we have read) must be eliminated from the data that we 'acquire' rules from, whereas other sentence patterns that only occur in the spontaneous speech of our interlocutors will be accepted as appropriate data. We may accept as probable that spontaneous speech is more likely to provide us with usable input (and it will certainly provide us with more in a shorter time than constructed speech), but what possible kind of evidence could be adduced for the claim that constructed speech cannot or will not be accepted as relevant data for creative construction?

Again, what exactly is meant by a 'learned system'? Krashen usually writes as if it will involve a conscious, even painstaking application of rules, in which constructing a sentence is consciously planned, and publicly explicable. But conscious application may take many forms. How would Krashen classify the concentrated study of Lorca poems recorded by a native speaker of Spanish: 'Many of my private vocabulary words came from these poems' (Savignon, 1981: 749)? And why does Rivers refer in her diary to combining concentrated conscious learning with communicative groping for words with anyone who would talk to her (Rivers, 1979)?[9] If Krashen seriously intends the statement that learned material can only contribute to monitoring, but monitoring requires time and a commitment to formal correctness – a claim that he reiterates – then are we to assume that Rivers' conscious effort is wasted except perhaps insofar as she intended to produce written messages in formal prose?

Unless there is some connection between acquisition and learning, many informed and skilled language users have wasted a great deal of their own and their students' time. Of course this does not in itself constitute an objection, but to fly so firmly in the face of so well-established a tradition requires a very strong basis of research evidence. Yet the research position on this is confusing. Even if we accept the claim that 'there is as yet no counter evidence to the hypothesis that the existence of the natural order in the adult is indeed a manifestation of the creative construction process, or language acquisition' (Krashen, 1978: 8), this does not entail a concurrent claim that no learning processes can have been used by learners in the course of acquisition. The natural order claim is about production and intuition about production, not about the processes causing production – Krashen's distinction simply gives a name to two black boxes and calls such baptisms an explanation. In order to falsify the claim as it stands, it is only necessary to produce learners who have attained a high level of potential fluency by orthodox, self-conscious learning – anyone, for example, who has learnt a language from a teach-yourself book. Krashen will have to argue that their language use must be limited to what they have encountered in natural circumstances. He has tried to avoid this difficulty by arguing that extensive reading constitutes normal input (Krashen, 1982: 164–5), but here again there are problems in determining the relations between the struggling through a book in a foreign language with a dictionary and occasional recourse to a grammar, and the gradually developing speed and automaticity which may be encountered even before one book has been completed. Yet Krashen is consistently dismissive (though he tries to avoid giving this impression) of conscious learning. Even when he addresses himself specifically to 'some benefits of conscious learning', the only justifications he can produce are that

1 for optimal monitor users there can be a real increase in accuracy;
2 conscious learning can teach about language for those who like linguistics;
3 over users of the monitor can be given confidence in the creative construction process by being given rules which confirm their already acquired intuitions.
                                                              (Krashen, 1978: 25–6)

This is not an impressive list, and it begs several questions. We may ask, for example, whether a 'real increase in accuracy' makes sense as a concept independently of communicative acts; why automatic monitoring should not be fostered for learners in relation to the communicative acts in which they participate; and what the relationship is between 'acquisition' and *automatic* monitoring such as we all acquire to a greater or lesser extent.[10] Furthermore, as Sajavaara has pointed out (1978: 56–9), monitoring is characteristic of mother-tongue speech as well as foreign-language speech. Indeed, some degree of self-consciousness is necessary for any self-regulating activity, and some natural monitoring will be a prerequisite for the operation of Grice's co-operative principle to occur, so Krashen's position, in a strong form, is not really compatible with natural language use at all.

The problem is that he appears to have made at least two unjustified confusions. First, he identifies conscious learning with the conscious learning (by heart?) of *rules* of grammar, when audiolingual procedures on S–R bases, on the one hand, or effort to learn a text by heart, on the other, may both be equally conscious learning, but without explicit concern with cognitive attention to rules. Second, he identifies the process of monitoring with the careful, piece-by-piece, conscious application of rules. It is trivial simply to say that you cannot use a language if you cannot produce automatic appropriate responses, but much of Krashen is no more than a scholarly reiteration of this truism. A much more important question is how the monitor relates to language use, rather than whether it does. Even if we cannot answer this question precisely, we can make use of the experience of learners and teachers in using the research literature surveyed by Krashen more appropriately for the classroom.

It may be, then, that a weak version of Krashen's position will have some value. But such a version, which states simply that self-conscious language production is not necessarily engaging identical processes as unself-conscious language production, and that the two processes, if there are two, interact with each other, is lacking in explanatory power, and is indistinguishable from versions proposed by Bialystok (1978), McLaughlin (1978b), and Stevick (1980), except insofar as the mechanisms proposed vary in each of these models. In its strong form, Krashen has the disadvantages of being confused or inexplicit on certain key issues (such as the definition of 'learning'), of being intrinsically unfalsifiable, of conflicting directly with the intuitions of successful language learners and successful language teachers, and of being merely descriptive with no explanatory power. In spite of the influence of his work, therefore, we cannot justifiably use it as a basis for language-teaching methodology.

Yet the five distinctions so far examined, as well as Stevick's and McLaughlin's models referred to above, do all reflect awareness of different activities or processes which require some examination. Even if the distinctions have been made for different purposes within different frames of reference, they do reflect a concern with similar phenomena. The accuracy/fluency distinction was also made in response to such concerns, and it is time to examine it more closely.

4 Accuracy and fluency

4.1 The basic polarity

In Chapter 1 we suggested that a legitimate procedure for the understanding of teaching was to move towards fundamental principles through the discussion of personal experience. In this section we shall exemplify that procedure. Consequently, it may be most helpful to start autobiographically, by referring to classroom experience.

I first began to formulate a distinction along these lines, though somewhat confusedly, in about 1968, when it became apparent that the highly controlled writing exercises I had helped to devise (illustrated in Broughton *et al.*, 1978: 121–31) conflicted with some of the educational and linguistic aims of the English course. The immediate consequence of this concern was to accept an *ad hoc* solution by allowing students to produce highly controlled writing, according to the scheme of exercises which had been devised, for some of the time, but at other times to encourage them to write freely and spontaneously – a diary or stories, for example – on the understanding that it would be read and discussed (or not if the writers preferred not), but that it need not be corrected. This strong division of function in the activities demanded of students arose from our recognition of the need for standard written English to be produced without so many errors that it would be demotivating to the writer (Bright and McGregor, 1970: 130–1), coupled with our perception from experience that such controlled writing never gave students the chance to produce in the early stages genuine, spontaneous text. We felt that they were being offered writing solely as a semi-conscious operation, with no construction of meaning as they wrote, only of form.[1] But at the same time we recognised the impossibility of expecting to use meaningful writing as a basis for correction, for that would impair the communicative relationship implicit in a text which is intended to be genuinely read. We were in fact already at that time using group discussion techniques extensively for all aspects of our work (as in Munby, 1968) and advocating such techniques for widespread use in secondary schools in Tanzania (Isaacs, 1968). Later, it seemed apparent that an educational principle was visible throughout the language and literature teaching that we were engaged in: a principle of allowing people to operate as effectively as they could, and attempting to adjust or mould what they produced in the desired direction, rather than explicitly teaching and expecting convergent imitation. Only retrospectively did I become aware that this principle not only underlies much of the more active language-teaching methodology, but also my own practice in teaching literature to native or non-native speakers and in training language teachers.

It is not being claimed here that the procedure adopted was particularly unusual or original. Nor, of course, does it overcome the problem of how to start teaching with new learners. But it does illustrate an awareness, based on classroom practice and teaching intuition rather than theory or research data, of a conceptual polarisation similar to those already examined. In this respect it resembles Rivers' skill-getting/skill-using distinction most closely, though it differs from that in having been based more specifically on a reduction of teaching input, so that the teacher responded rather than initiated – a course 'which expands the student's existing knowledge of the language not by necessarily adding any items at all, but simply by aiming to produce complete accuracy in the areas with which he is already familiar' (Brumfit, 1971: 32).

From this direct concern with a teaching need came an increasing awareness that, particularly for language work but arguably for most learning, the demand to produce work for display to the teacher in order that evaluation and feedback could be supplied conflicted directly with the demand to perform adequately in the kind of natural circumstances for which teaching was presumably a preparation. Language display for evaluation tended to lead to a concern for accuracy, monitoring, reference rules, possibly explicit knowledge, problem solving and evidence of skill-getting. In contrast, language use requires fluency, expression rules, a reliance on implicit knowledge and automatic performance. It will on occasion also require monitoring and problem-solving strategies, but these will not be the most prominent features, as they tend to be in the conventional model where the student produces, the teacher corrects, and the student tries again.

The emphasis in making the accuracy/fluency distinction is on the mental set of the learner. If the language is being produced for display purposes, the learner is intended to produce examples of language according to the requirements of the teacher, who may be demanding phonological, syntactic, lexical, functional, or stylistic convergence on a norm which may or may not have been specified. Whatever the conditions, the learner is expected to demonstrate usage, not use (Widdowson, 1978a: 3–4), and will adopt strategies accordingly. If such strategies are inappropriate for some or all of the activities involving natural language use, their encouragement in the classroom needs careful justification. At the same time, the arguments for a substantial proportion of the time being spent on activities which do involve natural language use require careful examination also. In principle, if we can show that accuracy-aimed activities do feed in to language acquisition, we could decide that that is sufficient, arguing that using the system comes naturally to those who have acquired it. But the evidence we have reviewed in Chapter 2 does not support this view,[2] so we need to look at the role of genuine language use in the classroom, and the extent to which it can ever be really genuine.

The distinction between accuracy and fluency is essentially a methodological distinction, rather than one in psychology or linguistics. That is to say, it is a division which may have value to teachers in decision making about the content of lessons and the distribution of time between various types of activity. Its value in communicative language teaching will be technological rather than theoretical, in that it is a distinction which is being made with the intention of producing better teaching – teaching which is as close as possible to our understanding of the nature of language and of language acquisition. We may recognise that the distinction is not absolutely tidy, just as we recognise the existence of self-monitoring and correction in the fluent speech of many proficient language users. But the justification for formulating the distinction in this way lies in the potential accessibility of the formulation to teachers who may not have either the time or the inclination to participate in careful theoretical analysis. This issue will be discussed in more detail later.

Accuracy

What is meant by the term 'accuracy' is not generally problematic. It reflects a concern that has always been strong in the history of language teaching, which will result in usage, rather than use of language in the classroom.[3] The only points about the term 'accuracy', as used here, that require clarification are the following:

1 In no sense is it meant to imply that fluent language may not also be accurate language; it simply refers to a focus by the user, because of the pedagogical context created or allowed by the teacher, on formal factors or issues of appropriacy, which will be evaluated for their observed characteristics rather than ignored (as they would be in normal discourse) except insofar as they impede satisfactory completion of the discourse.

2 The distinction is not one between what is good and bad in language teaching; it will be argued that there is a definite role for accuracy work in language teaching, but that its function is quite different from that of fluency work, and its over-use will impede successful language development.

3 Since 'accuracy' here refers to a focus of the user, it can refer just as much to listening and reading as to speaking and writing; any language activity which is not being carried on with the learners apparently

operating in the same way as they do in natural, mother-tongue use is an accuracy activity. Thus, extensive reading is aimed at fluency but much intensive reading work is aimed at accuracy; free and some situational writing exercises are aimed at fluency but all controlled and much guided writing is aimed at accuracy; listening exercises are aimed at accuracy but casual listening in the classroom has a major role as a fluency activity.

4 The 'quality' of the language produced or of comprehension is irrelevant to the distinction; language work focused predominantly on language is always accuracy work, however 'fluently' it may be performed, whereas language work which entails using the target language as if it is a mother tongue is always fluency work – the accuracy or inaccuracy of the language produced is irrelevant, and so also is the halting or tentative nature of the language process; the criterion is always the intended mental set of the user.

5 Just as native speakers monitor, so monitoring may take place during fluency work, but only if it has the same intention as it has for native speakers. However, it is recognised that the value of the distinction for teachers should not lead them to prevent learners, particularly at intermediate and advanced levels, from combining a concern with language use with worry about formal accuracy in terms of specific language items; pedagogical self-monitoring can be regarded as accuracy intervening in fluency activity, but making the distinction does not force us to prevent such intervention if learners want it – though this should not be recommended as the prime learning strategy.

Fluency

The term 'fluency', in contrast, raises more difficulties. This is partly because, whereas 'accuracy' is here being used with a meaning close to the common one (except insofar as it embraces appropriacy as well), 'fluency' is used with slightly different implications. Furthermore, even in common usage, 'fluency' is difficult to define, though it is a term which has been used for a long time with reference to language teaching (see Crystal, 1971: 47–51, for a discussion of some of the ambiguities, and also of the notion of 'receptive fluency'). The nature of 'fluency' as here contrasted with 'accuracy' has been indicated in the discussion of 'accuracy' above, but it will be useful to relate the concept as used here to discussions of the concept in conventional linguistic work, before examining its role in teaching methodology.

C.J. Fillmore (1979), discussing fluency with exclusive reference to production, distinguishes four different kinds. The first is 'the ability to fill time with talk', to talk without significant pauses for an extended period. For this ability to develop, monitoring must be unconscious or automatic, and the quality of the talk is less important than the quantity. The second kind is 'the ability to talk in coherent, reasoned and "semantically dense" sentences', showing a 'mastery of the semantic and syntactic resources of the language'. Chomsky is one of the examples given. Fillmore's third kind is 'the ability to have appropriate things to say in a wide range of contexts', so that you do not become tongue-tied with strangers or lost for words when an unexpected situation arises. And his fourth is the ability to be 'creative and imaginative in . . . language use', including punning, joking, varying styles, creating metaphors, etc.: 'the impression you have with this kind of speaker is that he does very rapid preediting of what he says, that he is quickly able to look over a large range of alternative ways of responding to a situation and chooses the one that sounds most sonorous or clever'. 'The maximally gifted wielder of language', Fillmore maintains, 'is somebody who has all of these abilities' (all quotations from C.J. Fillmore, 1979: 93).

These characteristics relate respectively to speed and continuity, coherence, context-sensitivity, and creativity. The basic sets of abilities required will be, respectively, psycho-motor, cognitive (perhaps relatable to Halliday's 'mathetic' function), affective (perhaps relatable to Halliday's 'pragmatic' function),[4] and aesthetic. What they clearly represent is a set of abilities that language users possess to varying degrees, but all of which they will require to some extent if they are to operate effectively as social communicators. One key question is the extent to which they can truly be considered linguistic abilities, for with the exception of the first they all require capacities which we recognise in people who are not linguistically fluent. The ability to marshal arguments cogently and present them with maximum skill may exist in someone who can do this only after successive redraftings; the ability to respond sensitively and appropriately to varying situations and circumstances may be possessed, and demonstrated, by people who are not verbally fluent but who express themselves primarily through non-verbal means, by sympathetic expressions and gestures, by subtle judging of how much or how little physical contact to make, and so on; and creativity in language use has some relationship to the ability to establish significant relationships between concepts, visual and aural patterns and systems of thought – the creativity is expressed through the language, and not merely within the linguistic system. In other words, Fillmore's categories seem to relate to an interaction between the language system that we operate and other personality characteristics. Fluency, in these senses, will not be promoted by language activities independent of other kinds of educational activities. It should also be noted that all of these types of fluency can be treated receptively as well as productively; but to respond to wit or coherence we shall have to know about the subject matter, and to recognise appropriacy we shall have to 'read' or interpret the complex interplay of a range of signalling systems, which will not be solely linguistic.

Fillmore's discussion is extremely helpful because it draws attention to the interaction between language and knowledge of the world in the development of fluency. The same cannot be said of Leeson's book-length study (1975). He defines fluency as 'the ability of the speaker to produce indefinitely many sentences conforming to the phonological, syntactical and semantic exigencies of a given natural language on the basis of a finite exposure to a finite corpus of that language' (Leeson, 1975: 136). The problem, from the point of view of our argument, is that Leeson operates with an idealised competence model which prevents him from departing from analyst categories, and causes him to concentrate exclusively on fluency as describable by linguists. The implicit pedagogy, (revealed in chapter 7 of his book), is entirely based on accuracy as it has been defined above. Consequently the 'factors in fluency' that Leeson identified (his chapter 6), such as breathing control, the learning of generative rules, and so on, constitute a description of part of what a language learner has to do, without any reference to the ways in which language is actually learned; for the discussion of language acquisition (pp. 8–12) takes no account of situational interaction, and is primarily concerned with phonology and 'the acquisition of the fundamental "rules" of a language' as distinct from 'later refinements in terms of range of lexis and stylistic subtleties which will be seen to be factors of performance rather than elements of fundamental competence in the language' (Leeson, 1975: 9). It is clear that such a formulation ignores precisely those 'performance' elements which will contribute to acquisition if we take the creative construction hypothesis seriously.

The model of language learning that underlies Leeson's work is in direct conflict with that outlined in Chapter 2 of this book. Such an approach still has adherents, though. The model of language work outlined in Rosenbaum (1973: 18–19), for example, assumes that much of the class's activity will be production of language to be checked for errors by 'a teacher who is a competent speaker of the language', because 'the foreign language student left to his own devices may not be aware that he has made an error, or he may not know where his error occurred, or what it was'. P.D. Smith states that 'second language learning – and perhaps also first language learning – involves four fundamental processes: (1) *presentation* to the learner of the new material, (2) *explanation* to the learner of the meaning and form of the new material, (3) *repetition* of the new material until it is learned, and (4) *transfer* of the new material to other contexts by the learner' (P.D. Smith, 1981: 21). We need not deny the value of such work, at least for some foreign-language learners, and it would fit as part of our accuracy work. But it should be clear from our previous discussion that such activity may not be necessary for everyone, and certainly is not sufficient for anyone. The Rosenbaum position, in particular, is unexpected, as it comes as part of an experiment to enable students to take more responsibility for their own learning; but it is clear that the instructional model still has its attractions and must be taken into account in any attempt to improve teaching methodology. However, its limitations as a classroom interpretation of language-learning strategies must also be clear.

Fluency, then, is to be regarded as natural language use, whether or not it results in native-speaker-like language comprehension or production. What are the important aspects of such natural language use which distinguish it from traditional classroom activity? Working within the constraints imposed by classrooms – intending, that is, to emulate native-speaker use of language in similar settings – we can identify a number of important differences.

1 Language produced should have been processed by the speaker, or comprehension should have been constructed by the reader or listener, without being received verbatim from an intermediary.

2 The content should be determined by the speaker or writer, though, of course, in relation to the demands of the specific task. This may require response to content determined by other members of the class, or by a teacher or textbook. ('Content' here refers to the subject matter, the topic of discourse, not as in some discussions of language teaching to the language items being focused upon.)

3 Normal processes of adjustment to the demands of a changing situation will be necessary – thus, in speech, improvising, paraphrasing, repair and reorganisation will frequently occur, and in reading, scanning ahead and rereading will be expected strategies. Listening to formal speeches, such as lectures, which cannot be interrupted, poses greater problems, which will require a separate programme, where appropriate.

4 The objective of the activity should be quite distinct from the formation of appropriate or correct language – the language will always be a means to an end.

5 Students should not normally be aware of intervention by the teacher as teacher rather than as communicator during the performance of the activity. This has implications for the power relations in the class, but the crucial point is that the teacher's unavoidably greater power to determine what is or is not appropriate behaviour should not affect students' freedom to hide or reveal their own intimate feelings, or personal information, in the same way as they would be free to choose in a non-pedagogic environment. It also has implications for our attitude to error. Correction should have either no place, or a very minor place, in fluency work, for it normally distracts from the message, or may even

be perceived as rude. In fact (as Corder, 1975, makes clear), error will be an inevitable part of the process of second-language development, and the behaviourist view that errors inevitably reinforce errors must be modified in the light of the research findings of the last twenty years (see also discussion in H.D. Brown, 1981: 116–17).

Fluency, then, can be seen as the maximally effective operation of the language system so far acquired by the student.[5] The claim is that by putting students into positions where the demands of the situation force them to use language as fluently as possible (in this sense of fluency), the process of creative construction should be assisted. The extreme interpretation of this position – that problem-solving activities using English can completely replace formal instruction in English – will be discussed in relation to the Bangalore Project in Chapter 6. Here, we shall consider activities designed to promote accuracy and activities designed to promote fluency as complementary in the language-teaching programme. However, in order to justify this position, it is necessary to examine the relationship between learning and teaching in conventional school systems.

4.2 Learning and teaching

In an interesting linguistic analysis, Halliday has explored relations between language and the real world with reference to the sentence 'The teacher taught the student English', and has suggested five separate possible analyses (Halliday, 1976). These can be summarised as follows:

	THE TEACHER	TAUGHT	THE STUDENT	ENGLISH
1	*actor*	*process*	*beneficiary*	*goal*
	'The teacher	imparted	the student	English.'
cf.	Peter	gave	Paul	a penny.
2	*actor*	*process*	*goal*	*range*
	'The teacher	instructed	the student	in English.'
cf.	Peter	beat	Paul	at ping pong.
3	*initiator*	*process*	*actor*	*range*
	'The teacher	caused to learn	the student	English.'
cf.	Peter	got to practise	Paul	palmistry.
4	*initiator*	*process*	*cognizant*	*range*
	'The teacher	enabled to know	the student	about English.'
cf.	Peter	interested	Paul	in politics.

5	*initiator*	*process*	*speaker*	*range*
	'The teacher	enabled to become a speaker	the student	of English.'

(Halliday, 1976: 347–8)

There is no comparable example for the fifth analysis because 'a feature of this analysis is that it applies rather specifically to just this kind of process, namely "teach + language", which it interprets as, in effect, unique' (Halliday, 1976: 348).

This linguistic exercise not only illustrates conveniently the range of possible relationships implicit between teacher and student, but it also – and this is, of course, its prime intention – shows that 'behind the *linguistic* semiotics (i.e. the semantics) of this sentence lies the semiotics of the language teaching process' (Halliday, 1976: 349). What is significant in this analysis for our purposes is the distinction between actor and initiator. We can observe the teacher operating in examples 1 and 2, but our recognition of the other three will depend on observation of the student, not of the teacher. We thus have an extension and clarification of Scheffler's paradigm cited in 1.2 (Scheffler, 1960), which specifically relates it to the requirements of language teaching. But built into the relationship between the teacher and the student is a disjuncture. Whereas the process in the first two examples is overt and consequently verifiable, in the last three it is covert: teachers certainly *intend* to cause or enable students to do things, but whether they actually succeed is extremely difficult to test, because there may be many other reasons why students develop, apart from teaching (see the discussion of Long, 1982, later in this chapter, for some evidence on the contribution of instruction to language development). Thus it is possible to separate teaching from learning in several important ways.

The total process of teaching is a complex phenomenon which will depend to varying degrees not only on the specific pedagogical behaviours of teachers, but also on the administrative and social context of their activity, on their personal attitudes and habits, and on the collective expectations of their students. But teaching is an institutionalised activity in a way that learning cannot be, so that it is possible to identify and intervene in the formal teaching process with some precision, for there are conventional sets of behaviour which constitute approved practice for teachers of particular subjects. It is such conventional sets of behaviour that are customarily developed in teacher training institutions, exemplified in textbooks and syllabuses, and debated in professional journals. The characteristics which set teaching apart from learning spring mostly from the fact that these behaviours can be observed, adapted, and evaluated. The important differences for our argument are summarised below.

	Teaching	*Learning*
1	causative by intention	may occur willingly or unwillingly
2	consists of a linear sequence of observable events	is internal and unobservable

hence:

	can be:	cannot be:
3	planned	
4	directly related to conscientious effort	
5	based on a syllabus	
6	observed, evaluated, and accredited to create a 'profession'	
7	administratively controlled	

but:

8	effectiveness in normal conditions cannot be measured.	effectiveness can be measured by observation of subsequent performance.

If we accept this position, then it makes sense to see what the teacher does as something that contributes to learning, but it certainly does not make sense to see teaching as simply the obverse of learning. Thus, while teaching strategies need to take into account their relationship with learners' potential strategies, there is no sense in which they can mirror these directly. This is partly because learner strategies have a wide range of variation that we cannot possibly predict (see, for example, Stern, Wesche and Harley, 1978: 434), and partly because of the necessity to allow learners the freedom to create their own grammars. The teacher's traditional function may be seen as analogous to that of the textbook writer: that is, as a presenter of language as tokens to the learner. This is what occurs when the presentation and formal practice activities of traditional teaching are being operated, and also when the teacher is correcting the student's output or comprehension. These are all aspects of the teacher's activity that can be guided and planned, but the direct relationship between these and the process of learning remains obscure. Allwright (1976) classifies these as 'samples' and 'guidance', but adds a third analytical category – 'management activities' – which may interact with these two; indeed, formal practice activities specifically interweave the provision of samples with management activities. But the last category may become much more important when we leave the role of the teacher as a provider of tokens and regard it as an activating role, in the sense of Halliday's analyses 3, 4, and 5. Then the choice of activities will become even more important, but the guidance role will disappear altogether, and the provision of sample language will be drastically reduced. Further-more, the teacher's role as a teacher in the sense outlined above will have to be modified; learning will be dependent partly on the teacher's ability to stop teaching and become simply one among a number of com-municators in the classroom. Without such an ability, teachers will prevent their learners from ever having the opportunity to convert tokens that have been formally 'learnt' into communicative systems that have been 'acquired' (using these terms to represent simply conscious and unconscious learning respectively).

4.3 An interim model of the language-teaching process

We are now in a position to summarise the argument so far, and to present an interim model of language teaching. If such a model is to have any value, it must recognisably belong to the world of language teachers as they are, for we are concerned with teaching as an observable, and train-able, phenomenon. At the same time it must be compatible with our understanding of the nature of language, the processes of language acquisition or learning, and the social and psychological characteristics of teachers and learners. But since it is a model of *teaching* – that is, a model of principled intervention into these other areas – it must be a model which will not distort the characteristics of individual students. It must not be the effect of a teaching model that it forces learners to operate inefficiently, unless it can be shown with considerable confidence that making a few learners operate inefficiently will greatly increase the efficiency of the others – and even this view rests on an educational premiss that many would dispute. Since the role of a teaching model is to clarify our understanding (and therefore, we would hope, the efficiency) of the process of teaching, it is not advisable that it should incorporate hypothetical speculations about what we do not understand. Its function is not to account for how people acquire languages, but to indicate how teachers' activities can best assist that complex process. Insofar as we are operating with teaching, we shall have to be subject only to the social mechanisms of institutional and professional feedback (discussed in 1.3); consequently, the model must describe the nature of language acquisition *as seen by the teacher in the classroom*, and needs to be in sufficient detail only to enable teachers to improve their practice with reference to its basic categories.

This last point requires some explanation, for it is important for our position. We are attempting to produce a model for the language-teaching process, and this should represent a conceptual framework within which teachers can usefully operate. On the one hand, such a model should be compatible with current views of the nature of language and language acquisition; on the other, it should be sufficiently simple, realistic, and practicable to be developed into convenient classroom practice. In other words, it is a model of language acquisition tied to a view of teaching, and thus directly relating to our discussion in Chapter 1 of appropriate sources for an understanding of teaching.

In this section, then, we shall summarise the argument, building on the references and discussion in Chapter 2, and then outline a more speculative extension of the position illustrated by the model, in order to relate language teaching more firmly to broader educational development.

Our starting point for formulating this model is the complexity of language use and language acquisition. Views of the major role which language must play in the subjective construction of our social relationships have led to an increased appreciation of the multiplicity of systematic perceptions which contribute to language comprehension and language use. Furthermore, the language user is seen to be actively engaged in the process of making meaning, and so is the young child both in the early and later stages of acquiring language. The same may be said of the second-language learner in immersion situations. Again, although the examination of human relationships through an interactional model is still in its infancy (Hinde, 1979), the complexity of complementary and reciprocal relationships is clear, and has been touched upon in studies of teachers and students (Brophy and Good, 1974) as well as in more general studies.[6] Learners approaching second languages vary considerably in the strategies they adopt, both in and out of formal classrooms, but most language-learning models allow for interaction between social contextualised language acquisition and decontextualised language learning. There remains, however, considerable room for disagreement on whether, or how, to train students specifically in particular aspects of communication, or whether simply to facilitate development by allowing opportunities for uncontrolled interaction with interlocutors or text.[7]

But, in spite of the implications of Krashen's position, there is no strong support for a rejection of formal teaching. Indeed, Long (1982) surveys thirteen studies which relate language acquisition to exposure or instruction, and concludes that from these 'there is considerable (although not overwhelming) evidence that instruction is beneficial (1) for children as well as adults, (2) for beginners, intermediate and advanced students, (3) on integrative as well as discrete-point tests, and (4) in acquisition-rich as well as acquisition-poor environments' (Long, 1982: abstract attached to p. 1). As Long points out, the implications of this seriously challenge the monitor model, which can be realistically salvaged only by broadening the concept of learning (though that would not avoid the objections raised above in Chapter 3), or by allowing learning to lead to acquisition (Long, 1982: 17–18). More striking, though, if we examine the available studies, is the lack of concern with the complexity of teaching. An examination of a number of studies reveals that only one considers in any detail the different types of language activity covered by the term 'instruction'. Nine studies (Upshur, 1968; Hale and Budar, 1970; Mason, 1971; Fathman, 1975; Brière, 1978; Chihara and Oller, 1978; Krashen, Jones, Zelinski, and Usprich, 1978; Martin, 1980; J.D. Brown, 1981) measure instruction against other variables, treating instruction purely quantitatively. Fathman (1976) does distinguish oral and written biases in class, and also individualised versus group instruction, but these are not distinctions which will reveal the 'natural' and 'pedagogic' styles of interaction or task as distinct from one another. Since the kind of distinction we have been making between accuracy and fluency in the classroom has immediate implications for language available for acquisition as against language arranged for learning, and since these studies are much cited in the literature (the early ones are all cited in Krashen, 1981a, for example), the simple view of teaching is to be regretted; indeed, it casts doubt on his (and other researchers') awareness of the nature of teaching.

Accepting, then, that we lack strong reasons for rejecting some elements of formal teaching, it makes sense to design a model which is both explicable in terms of the regular experience of teachers, and compatible with the need to allow communicative interaction a prominent place. From a model of this kind we can interpret descriptive psycholinguistic models (for example, Bialystok, 1978), but, equally, social-psychological ones (for example, Gardner, 1979); above all, it is capable of operating with the type of explanatory hypothesis put forward by Widdowson (1978b), which allows a motivation for the different types of test results examined by Krashen. For clarity, I shall present it in four phases, with a commentary following each phase.

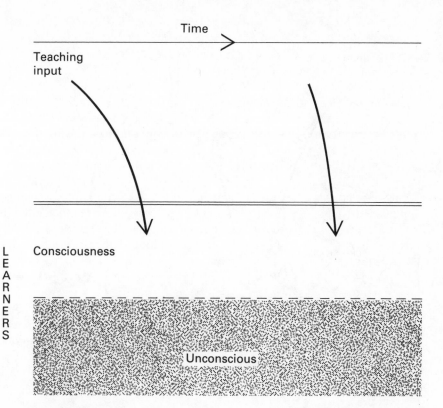

Fig. 1a Basic teaching

Imagine the model as a cross-section of the learners' internalising capacities, extended over time from left to right, with – above the double line – the public operations with language represented on the same time scale.

The first phase (Fig. 1a) illustrates the process of formal, accuracy-based teaching, and also that of all initial exposure to new language items. Presentation of new language, through talk, textbook, cassette or overt presentation techniques, together with specific correction by the teacher of any aspect of language, is covered by the arrows. We cannot legitimately assume that such teaching will necessarily have any immediate impact below the level of consciousness.

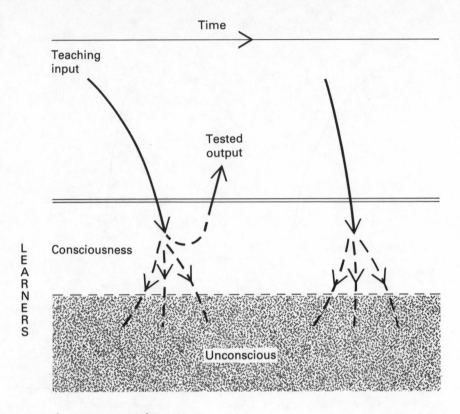

Fig. 1b   Conventional testing

The second phase (Fig. 1b) illustrates the conventional testing situation. Production has been frequently associated with specific teaching, but production for test purposes proceeds from learned abilities which may or may not have been assimilated to the underlying knowledge of the system of the language. Indeed, if testing follows too rapidly on teaching it may well only test unassimilated language items. This phase of the model enables us to distinguish what Krashen would want to call learned language from acquired language. Unlike Krashen's model, however, this allows for a connection, but not one that is specifiable, between conscious and unconscious knowledge.

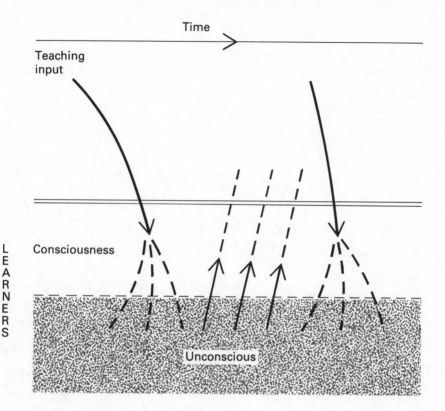

Fig. 1c   Language use

The third phase (Fig. 1c) illustrates the process of language use, whether productive or receptive, *as it appears from the position of the teacher.* In practice, there is no way of predicting a direct relationship between the provision of language data by the teacher, textbook, or casual contact with the target language, and the overt signs that the learner genuinely and spontaneously can either comprehend without effort or produce appropriately without effort. Some lexical items (for example, specific technical terms being used within a system with which the student is already familiar) may apparently become fully internalised almost at once. Many other items will be apparently usable only after months, or may never appear to be comprehended, or – more frequently – produced.

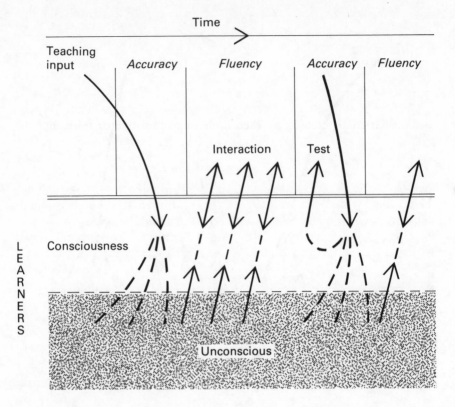

Fig. 1d Accuracy and fluency

The fourth phase (Fig. 1d) relates this model to the accuracy/fluency distinction. The contention is that an acceptance of the argument of this study so far should lead us to place heavy emphasis on fluency activities on the grounds that through these conversion of conscious knowledge to unconscious knowledge will be facilitated. Whether this may be because reference rules are more or less conscious while expression rules are rules of association and creation of schemata which are universally negotiable is not as yet provable, but that hypothesis would receive considerable support if language teaching heavily based on fluency proved to be successful in normal educational systems.

4.3 An interim model of the language-teaching process

This model is extremely simplified because it needs to be both convincing and compatible with our somewhat uncertain knowledge. Jackson reports that highly respected teachers have uncomplicated views of the nature of causality, intuitive rather than rational approaches to classroom events, and opinionated rather than open-minded attitudes to teaching practices other than their own. He also points out that such views may be necessary in order to survive the 'ambiguity, unpredictability and occasional chaos created by each hour of twenty-five or thirty not-so-willing learners' (Jackson, 1968: 149). A lack of concern for the refinements of conceptual clarification may have to be part of the working equipment of a career teacher, but we do not have to be either patronising or pessimistic to concede that models for teaching methodology will not be effective within the profession if they are either incomprehensible to most teachers or incompatible with how learning takes place.

This concludes the initial description of the model. Its implications will be developed in the next chapter. As it stands, it enables us to consider a methodology of communicative language teaching, closely related to recent views on second-language acquisition. But there is also a stronger position that I wish to suggest in this study. Following Popper, research and the development of knowledge can be seen as a process of operating agreed conventions for the attempted solutions of agreed problems. Such a description would, if we follow the general trend of linguistic work of the past decade, also apply to the nature of language. It is also frequently maintained by educational philosophers that the development of new ideas and concepts is to a great extent the development of a new language (Langford, 1968: 37; Hirst, 1974: 83). But this position may also be inverted (Widdowson, 1968, 1975) to suggest that the development of a new language should be associated with the development of new ideas and concepts. This may be based not on the conventional view in which learning the ideas of the target culture is built into the course, but on a view of the nature of language in which the development of the linguistic system independent of new concepts would be analogous to the development of the ability to drive, independent of roads to drive along; the feeling of running through new territory is an essential part of the motivation and development of driving, and also of language.

Support for such a view can be found in contemporary German philosophy. Apel writes (1976: 58–9):

Are not the different syntactico-semantical systems or types of deep grammar *different ways* of a possible formation of a consensus about rules of the use of words, so that it a priori makes no sense to expect or postulate an *universal* consensus about questions of meaning-rules and thus about questions of 'essence'? The *relativistic* tendency of these objections is enforced, so it seems, by the consideration that the attempts, so far undertaken, to construct an ideal language of science did not lead to a *lingua universalis sive philosophica*, as it was postulated by Leibniz, but rather have reconfirmed the assumption of an a priori existing pluralism of possible 'semantical frameworks'. This result seems to be in harmony with the *conventionalism* and *pluralism* of *theories* or *paradigms* as it is recently defended as ultima ratio in the philosophy of science.

Having made the link with philosophies of science (and there is an explicit reference to Popperian views in a footnote), Apel considers the relations between language behaviour and language systems. He concludes (p. 60):

As it seems to me, the most important conclusion suggested by the history of understanding between human civilizations aims at a simultaneous distinction and dialectical mediation between *syntactico-semantical* language-*systems* and *semantico-pragmatic* language-*games*. While it may be possible to think of language-*systems* – especially if they are idealized according to the paradigm of artificial frameworks – as incommensurable conditions . . . of possible concept-formation, this view is obviously misleading with regard to language-*games* – if these are understood as pragmatical units of communication or social interaction.

If we sympathise with this view, if we see the process of second-language learning as one of learning to play language games, some of which we know already, with the tokens of a new language, then we cannot operate a methodology based on the assumptions of comparative language systems. Directions which are only beginning to be explored (see, for example, Giddens's, 1982, discussion of Habermas's ideas), in which knowledge and language systems interact as conventional resources for co-operation, will become increasingly important for language teaching. But for the moment, we must concentrate on the two preliminary issues of establishing a genuine interactive pattern in classrooms and maintaining some kind of serious conceptual development.

5 The bases for fluency activity: small-group work and a 'natural' linguistic environment

5.1 Classroom organisation

In the last chapter we suggested that accuracy activity may be aimed at conscious learning by students, but that the conversion of the tokens of the language thus learnt into value-laden systems with genuine communicative potential requires fluency activity in which the learners' focus is on meaning rather than form. Such a focus on meaning has implications for the organisation of the classroom and the activities demanded of students. These implications will be examined in this chapter.

The aim of fluency activity is to develop a pattern of language interaction within the classroom which is as close as possible to that used by competent performers in mother tongue in normal life. Since much language use is informal, small-group conversation, this will often involve students in participating in small groups of varying sizes. But it will also involve relating genuinely to written texts, and to other modes of communication in which feedback is dependent mainly on the receiver, such as recordings and broadcasts, and formal face-to-face interactions, such as lectures and speeches.

Redefining the 'four skills'

Since the emphasis in fluency activity is on successful and relaxed operation with the language, one fundamental piece of rethinking is necessary. Traditional teaching and teacher training have based themselves firmly on the 'four skills' of listening, speaking, reading, and writing. While this classification has some value if we look at language activity from the outside, in practice most teaching finds itself compromising by combining skills (or operating a separate activity called 'integrated skills'), and the definition of language implied by this division ignores the function of language altogether; the four categories describe things which happen, but only as external, discrete, unmotivated activities. If we feel that fluency activity should enable learners to develop their capacities as closely as possible to the ways in which current language acquisition theory sees language as developing, we require a different specification of objectives. This specification would recognise the interconnections

69

between the activities described by the traditional four skills and be capable of being related more closely to function and purpose.

There seem to be three major isolable activities in language work for most students:

i) conversation, or discussion;
ii) comprehension (either of speech or writing);
iii) extended writing.

A fourth activity, 'extended speaking', may be added in appropriate circumstances, probably at advanced levels, but it is not an activity that all native speakers actually use or require, and can be treated as an independent problem. (These distinctions resemble fairly closely those of Breen and Candlin, 1980: 92, between 'negotiation', 'interpretation', and 'expression', but they regard these as underlying abilities, which are not necessarily even linguistic – note 6, their p. 109 – while the purpose here is to integrate such abilities with linguistic behaviour so that classroom activities can be seen to serve one of these three, or four, goals.)

The argument for reclassifying the 'four skills' in this way is, first, that the new classification integrates each activity with communication, whereas the listening/speaking distinction particularly separates activities which are often in practice simultaneous and interdependent, and, second, that it focuses attention on meaning rather than on the analysable formal elements. The traditional emphasis on the 'four skills' has frequently reduced 'writing' to a concern with handwriting and transfer of spoken to written form with little attention to discourse structure, and 'listening' to a concern with minimal pairs or comprehension of isolated sentences. This alternative proposal also corresponds to common-sense assessments of what we do with language, in that each of the four activities listed is observably different from the others, and requires response to different conventions; while at the same time there is a sense in which we perceive ourselves to stop doing one of them and start doing another – they can be seen as, in principle, independent modes of behaviour.

The only area which is likely to be particularly contentious is the inclusion of the comprehension of speech and writing together, but the separation of extended production of each of them. There is, in fact, increasing evidence that the distinction between spoken and written forms is not as important as the choice of content or genre (Tannen, 1982) in the organisation of continuous text. (This may be intuitively recognised by teachers in the long-standing tradition of combining oral and written stimulation as part of the process of grading comprehension for class use – see, for example, Broughton *et al.*, 1978: 108.) On the other hand, the process of production of extended text is dominated by personal and social factors when the medium is oral, and these require separate treatment from the process of planning a speech, which does not differ greatly from that of drafting an extended written text. The planning of extended speaking may be treated as a development from the planning of extended writing (or vice versa in some cultures), but it is a development which not all students will make use of, and which requires careful attention to problems of projection as well as organisation, so that it is best left as an independent activity.

Let us turn, then, to the problem of the development of a context for conversation, or discussion activity, for the abilities required to produce language in the larger context of the full class may be quite different from those needed in normal conversation. There are in addition, of course, a range of educational reasons for wanting small-group activity in the classroom. The ways in which pedagogical, linguistic, and broader educational criteria interact are complicated and worth examining in some detail, for our attitude to small-group teaching will affect other aspects of teaching, such as syllabus organisation and materials selection and design. 'Groups', incidentally, can include 'pairs' in this discussion, as the differences between these are not significant for our purposes.

5.2   Group-work activity in education

Conventionally, as Cortis has pointed out (1977: 1), Western education has been based on the deliberate creation of sub-groups, or school classes. Since the 1930s, however, there has been an increasing interest in interactions between teachers, or group leaders, and smaller groups, varying in size from three to fifteen persons. This movement developed partly from the concern to avoid authoritarian structures in schools and youth work – often a direct reaction to the political events of the 1930s, with a strong moral or even religious underpinning – and partly from the implications of progressive educational philosophies such as Dewey's (1916).[1]

The moralistic impulse may be observed in the writings of, for example, Slavson (1937) and Kilpatrick (1940), though in the latter it is already coupled with an opposition to the conditioning and drill models of learning associated with behaviourism. More scientifically, the classic study of Lewin, Lippitt and White (1939) of authoritarian and democratic styles of leadership, although it was based on youth clubs rather than schools, provided a major impetus for investigations of less directive ways of organising classrooms. Dewey's concern with the process of learning, rather than the content, provides the basis for an emphasis on group work as a more efficient way of teaching subject matter. The democratic impulse is based partly on a belief that authoritarian procedures inhibit learning, but also on a desire to create responsible and critical citizens. Both these trends come together frequently in claims that genuine learning can only result from an integration of cognitive and affective responses by the learner, and this fusion has been influential in the humanistic movement of the 1960s and 1970s in the United States, outside education in its formal manifestations (Rogers, 1969), within general education (Simon, Howe and Kirschenbaum, 1972), and in foreign-language teaching (Stevick, 1976, 1980).

One definition of humanistic education, based on student responses, sees it as sensitive, empathetic, loving, fair and flexible, assured, conscientious, tolerant, understanding, altruistic, lively, imaginative, zealous, enthusiastic, and durable (Maples, 1979); and a concern for such general, though desirable, qualities is manifest in specific discussions of group work within this tradition (Flynn and La Faso, 1972, for example). Schmuck and Schmuck (1971: 15–17) have traced the increasing research interest in groups as a means of developing social sensitivity, a trend which has been influential in higher education (Bramley, 1979), as well as in business education (C.L. Cooper, 1979). Such trends reflect an increasing concern with interpersonal relations, and a drift away from purely transactional models of education or industrial management. In education, they also reflect a concern with counselling and with the view of the teacher as social worker as well as imparter of knowledge, which in turn may result from the demand for advanced education for all groups of students and not just for the academically inclined.

If we are to make sense of these diverse traditions in establishing their relevance for language teaching, we shall need to examine the social characteristics of groups in relation to the model of language we have established.

Characteristics of groups

A group is usually defined as a number of people who interact with one another, who are psychologically aware of one another, and who perceive themselves to be a group (Sprott, 1958: 9; Schein, 1965: 81; Handy, 1976: 145–6).

Psychological groups, as defined above, may be formal or informal, but educationally the two types should be kept distinct, for they fulfil different functions. Formal groups are either more or less permanent with defined roles over a long period, or temporary but with the function of performing specific tasks. Such groups will have specified functions within the organisation of the school, and such functions may perhaps be exploited for language activity, although they cannot be created as the prime source of activity. Informal groups, however, will occur primarily for social purposes whenever people interact, and consequently will emerge in any class. The language and interaction patterns of informal groups will differ from those of formal groups, and – since language work is a preparation for informal rather than formal activities for most students in general classes – it is such groups which should be simulated most often in the classroom. Informal groups will change in normal life and cannot be regarded as permanent, but they will provide for certain psychological needs of their members during the period of their functioning. Schein (1965: 84–5) lists these as:

i)   affiliation needs – for friendship and support;
ii) means of developing, enhancing and confirming a sense of identity and maintaining self-esteem;
iii) a means of establishing and testing reality, by establishing consensus and thus security about the nature of the world;
iv) a means of increasing security and a sense of coping with external threats;
v)   a means of getting specific jobs done determined by the wishes and needs of the group members.

Such needs pose problems for the teacher, for they may conflict with the instrumental concerns of pedagogy. However, they need both to be recognised as potential causes of disfunction, and to be accepted as inevitable factors in group activity in situations where language will eventually be used; so that they can be seen as potential sources of strength, by being realistic, as well as of weakness, by conflicting with intended group functions.

Such psychological factors only operate, however, within a social framework, and such a framework will affect the interactions within the situation of the group. Argyle, Furnham, and Graham (1981: 6–9) identify a range of features to define social situations: goals, rules (in the sense of shared beliefs about appropriate behaviour), possible roles, a repertoire of acceptable elements in the situation, sequences of behaviour, shared concepts, environmental settings, specific language for particular situations, difficulties, and skills required. By examining such factors they arrive at basic rules appropriate for all social situations:

i)   make communication possible (cf. Grice, 1975);
ii) prevent withdrawal by other actors;
iii) prevent aggression;
iv) begin and end encounters.

And they add rules for all *verbal* communication:

i)   don't all speak together (except to help out the speaker – N. Ferguson, 1977);
ii) observe rules for adjacency pairs;
iii) observe specific rules for longer sequences (Argyle, Furnham, and Graham, 1981: 184–6; see also Brown and Levinson, 1978; R.A. Hudson, 1980: 106–19).

What is not clear from the studies with which these rules are associated is the extent to which teaching can merely facilitate the development of rule-systems, and the extent to which specific instruction may be necessary. Nonetheless, it is clear from all these studies that putting students into small groups in the classroom will both open up for them possibilities of interaction which are not normally available in a whole-class approach, and also make demands on them which – while they are difficult to specify precisely – will force a closer integration of language with social behaviour than would otherwise be possible, in a way compatible with our view of language acquisition and use.

At the same time, it is necessary to recognise that the pressures to conformity in groups may involve risks as well as gains. There is a considerable literature (for example, Asch, 1956; Milgram, 1963; 1965) showing that groups will act according to the norm established, even against the judgements of individual members, if there are strong enough social pressures, either within or outside the group: people tend to conform, often against their better judgement, rather than withstand group pressure. Part of the teacher's task may be to monitor group performance and to ensure that such pressures do not result in too great a divergence from target norms, by being ready to introduce appropriate remedial activity during accuracy work.

Another potential difficulty has been raised by Gahagan (1975: 122), who claims that the personal relations allegedly improved by 'relationship' groups such as those influential in humanistic education may benefit in this way only because the group has no other function, and that such groups may operate differently from goal-directed groups. Unless we have some understanding of the role of affective interaction in the co-operative solution of external problems, we shall risk confusing 'relationship' activity with 'problem-solving' activity in classroom work. However, there are also models of group activity which see it as primarily concerned with resolving contradictions between members in the solution of specified tasks (Gustafson *et al.*, 1981), thus integrating the two models. On this issue, the picture from research is confused.

What is clear from this is that any use of language by small groups in the classroom requires learners to operate with a great deal more than language alone, for other semiotic systems will come into play, and personal and social needs will be expressed and responded to, simply as a result of the presence of several human beings together for a co-operative purpose. But the ways in which these systems interact have not been systematised by researchers, and perhaps are incapable of systematisation: Argyle, Furnham, and Graham confess themselves unable to construct anything resembling a grammar of social interaction (1981: 212). Teachers thus have their options limited in providing instruction in this area. However, this need not prevent them facilitating student activity; and the view of language outlined in Chapter 2 may actually support the argument that we shall be better placed if we provide opportunities for small-group interaction through the medium of the target language than if we try to teach analytically the procedures for interaction.

However, we have to recognise that an insistence on the value of small-group work for language teaching conflicts with some strands in the educational tradition that we have been exploring in this chapter. At least one standard work on group work in schools specifically exempts languages from suitability for small-group activity on the grounds – which clearly conflict with the view of language outlined here – that they are not 'capacious' and divergent, but 'linear' and convergent (Kaye and Rogers, 1968: 125); and more recent writers see skill and knowledge acquisition as appropriate for individual and competitive activity, whereas co-operative activity is reserved for creative and problem-solving tasks (Johnson and Johnson, 1975: 62).[2] Nonetheless, if we accept a creative construction view of language, all the arguments that favour small-group activity for content subjects apply to language work, with minor modifications, particularly if we accept the position that language practice with the risk of errors in formal terms is not detrimental to progress in language acquisition.[3] The major impact of the creative construction hypothesis logically must be to undermine the behaviourist view that errors reinforce errors, as we saw in our discussion of the concept of fluency.

Once we accept that the teacher does not have to monitor and provide feedback for every utterance of the student, arguments for individualisation and peer mediation (Rosenbaum, 1973) can be converted, at least partially, to arguments for small-group activity.

Any use of group work will massively increase the likelihood, in large classes, of students both producing and receiving language. It will also contribute considerably to both cognitive and affective development, according to several surveys of the research literature (Abercrombie, 1970; Schmuck and Schmuck, 1971; Johnson and Johnson, 1975); indeed, group co-operative rather than individual competitive procedures are held by these researchers to reduce anxiety, increase awareness of possible solutions to problems, and increase commitment to learning. There does appear to be some confusion here, for more recent research suggests that some kinds of conflict in groups, providing it is resolved within the group, leads to high achievement and retention (Smith, Johnson, and Johnson, 1981). Only in drill-like activities, according to Johnson and Johnson (1975), is competition between students a more efficient means of getting a task performed by children.[4] However, in spite of the impressive agreement by theorists that group work is desirable, we should note a recent observation (Sands, 1981) that group work is rarely used by teachers; and that, when it is, the children are frequently working on their own in the groups (though this is with reference to content subjects and based on a fairly small sample) – a comment that raises issues for teacher training, and also for theorists and the ways in which they present their ideas.

5.3   Group work in foreign- and second-language learning

There have been many general discussions of the use of group work for language learning (Isaacs, 1968; Rivers, 1968: 202–6; Rowlands, 1972; Sprenger, 1973; Long, 1975), and the British Council has held many overseas seminars specifically to introduce the technique (Jolly and Early, 1974). Earlier discussion (for example, A.S. Hornby, 1955; Forrester, 1968) tended to concentrate on the use of group work to break down the size of the enormous classes encountered in India rather than on the necessity of small groups for any kind of natural language activity, so that it is seen more as a management device than as a means of developing communicative competence.

Probably the most coherent linguistic argument for group work has been advanced by Long (1975). He begins by pointing out that traditional lock-step classrooms do not cause natural linguistic behaviour because they encourage the following assumptions:

i)   the teacher initiates language exchanges;
ii)   the student's task is to respond to the teacher;
iii) the teacher judges whether the student's performance is acceptable;
iv)   these judgements are based on grammatical and phonological accuracy;
v)   the grammatical standard required is that of the mature adult native speaker.

(Long, 1975: 217)

Long makes the point that we have already discussed about talking time available to students once group work is adopted, but then goes on to discuss the quality of language, referring to the work of Barnes (1969) with mother-tongue speakers working in groups. Long comments – though ignoring the differences between first- and second-language activity – 'Release from the need for "accuracy at all costs" . . . and entry into the richer and more accommodating set of relationships provided by small group interaction allows development of the kind of personalised, creative talk for which, theoretically at least, most ESOL courses are endeavoring to prepare their learners' (Long, 1975: 219). The third advantage identified is related to the second, for it involves the uses of language ('to define, hypothesise, classify, promise, apologise, command, etc.'), and it is argued that these will emerge from the small-group discussion and the roles which learners will have to play in this.

This type of argument differs from earlier arguments in the first phase of group work recommendation in that it proceeds directly from a view (though Long does not state it explicitly) of the nature of language learning which is close to that outlined in Chapter 2. Nonetheless, although there has been much discussion of the advantages of group work, it still does not figure prominently in methodology texts (an exception being

Broughton *et al.*, 1978), and even an explicitly 'acquisition-based' approach to language learning (such as Terrell, 1977) makes no detailed reference to the methodological implications. But it is difficult to see by what other procedures natural conversation can be simulated in normal-sized classes.

The model of language teaching that we have presented thus requires us to go further than simply to use group work as a more intensive way of organising classroom practice. We have to see it as *linguistically* necess-ary. But much discussion of group teaching, especially in higher edu-cation, assumes a direct instructional model, perhaps with a teacher present for the whole of the time (Abercrombie, 1970; Simons and Squires, 1976). Ciotti (1969), for example, follows a careful analysis of the interactional possibilities of small groups for foreign-language teach-ing with a highly directed teaching model, moving from controlled to par-tially controlled to non-controlled activities, but in fact the total structure enables most of the language activity at the non-controlled stage to be pre-dicted. A similar model seems to underlie Jolly and Early's claim that presentation can most effectively take place in a full frontal class position, and group work used to assist practice, exploitation, and transfer activities (Jolly and Early, 1974: 1).

We have, then, a number of basic justifications for the use of small groups in language classrooms. Many of them would be worth recom-mending whatever the model of language acquisition or of instruction being followed. Small groups provide greater intensity of involvement, so that the quality of language practice is increased, and the opportunities for feedback and monitoring also, given adequate guidance and prep-aration by the teacher. The setting is more natural than that of the full class, for the size of the group resembles that of normal conversational groupings. Because of this, the stress which accompanies 'public' per-formance in the classroom should be reduced. Experience also suggests that placing students in small groups assists individualisation, for each group, being limited by its own capacities, determines its own appropriate level of working more precisely than can a class working in lock-step, with its larger numbers. Furthermore, co-operation may be seen as ideologically desirable, especially in educational systems which advocate socialist principles. Jolly and Early, writing for Yugoslavia, summarise this argument:

Psychologically, group work increases the intellectual and emotional partici-pation or involvement of the individual pupil in the task of learning a foreign language. Some pupils are more intelligent than others, while some (not necess-arily the same ones) are more gifted in learning languages, some pupils are out-going, communicative, extrovert personalities, while others are shy, withdrawn introverts. In small groups, all these types of learner can meet and mix, compen-sating for one another's strong points and deficiencies as language learners.

(Jolly and Early, 1974: 2)

All of these assertions may contribute to the value of group work, but they are not, for our discussion, the most important justifications. Insofar as group work enables us to produce fluency activity, as specified on page 56 above, it must be an important part of a communicative methodology. Because the small group simulates natural conversational settings more closely than any other mode of classroom organisation (if we include pair work with group work), it will combine most effectively all aspects of communication, learning, and human interaction referred to in the justifications cited above, in the most integrated, non-threatening, and flexible mode of class organisation available to the teacher. The teacher in a large class *cannot* control the language being used in all groups – in view of our argument, a virtue rather than a deficiency. The language produced will be by definition at the level of the students, but it will be socially constrained by the fact that the group is a social organisation, only imposed to the extent that compulsory education necessarily imposes social organisation. The teacher's involvement, since it will tend to arise from casual and more or less irregular 'visiting' rather than from predictable intervention at specific points in the development of the group's work, will be more limited to chatting than to teaching, and the language that will thus arise is likely to provide useful data for acquisition. We may argue, in fact, that group work may increase the efficiency of accuracy work, for the educational reasons outlined above, but that *fluency* work in conversation will be impossible without the adoption of a flexible small-group system.

We have, then, two potential roles for group-work activity. One is to increase the intensiveness of accuracy work – and this may also perform the function of giving learners experience of group activity in clearly organised systems, so that they become used to the concept and do not feel threatened by the greater freedom later to be afforded by fluency-based group activity. Below are a number of examples of this which have been observed in foreign-language classrooms.

1 The teacher has decided that a particular phoneme of English is causing difficulty – Spanish learners failing to produce /j/ in initial position, as in 'yes' – and takes time off from the plan to perform a rapid remedial drill chorally. This is immediately followed by the direction to practise saying 'yes' in pairs, one student speaking while the other monitors. After a few tries, the pairs reverse roles. The whole exercise takes about one minute.

2 The students are reading dialogues which include a number of question tags. In order to avoid an unnatural rise on the tags, with Indian pupils, the teacher has organised the class in groups of three, two participating in the dialogue, the third checking specifically for that one fault, and correcting where necessary. The students rotate their roles between the two parts of the dialogue and the person who monitors. The teacher, meanwhile, wanders around the groups overhearing and occasionally intervening.

3   Students, working in groups of four, read out in turn their answers to an exercise they have done for homework, to which the teacher has already rapidly explained the answers. At the end of each sentence a designated leader asks each of the other two students listening, 'Is it right?' and the text is marked according to the agreed answer. The teacher patrols the class, resolving conflicts, and preventing the conflicts from degenerating into genuine argument, by rapidly providing an authoritative answer.

4   The students play a game (or practise an exercise – the principle is the same) which has already been demonstrated in class. The language produced is restricted to certain formulae, though a certain ease may be attained by the process of repetition. Thus, in 'Happy Families', the formula 'Do you have Mr Bun the Baker?' may be repeated and adapted in an apparently natural fashion.

5   Students in pairs, threes or fours prepare an exercise on a structural item (the first conditional) to which they have just been introduced for the first time. The exercise involves filling in blanks, and they read out the answers in rotation. Later, after some oral preparation, they will be expected to write individually.

[Examples of group and pair work and accuracy]

These examples (all of which I have observed in various places) have been deliberately selected as examples lacking in a fluency dimension. It is, however, important to recognise that even this degree of teacher withdrawal is still rare in many foreign-language classrooms (Mitchell, Parkinson, and Johnstone, 1981: 32), and that utilisation of such techniques does give students something marginally closer to natural language activity than might otherwise have been attained – the quantity of target language production has been increased, and so probably has the spontaneity; the rapidity of feedback has been increased, and it may often be less threatening than when it comes from the teacher. But none of the requirements for fluency activity in my sense have in fact been realised. We should also note, though, that in practice the teacher in these circumstances often has to make some effort to prevent fluency activity taking place, in English in polyglot classes, in mother tongue in monolingual ones. All of these activities provide opportunities for explanation, and some of them cry out for discussion by students (no. 3, for example). It is unusual in practice for teachers not to have to limit discussion, and frequently discussion either in or partly in the target language, for some activities of this kind. As soon as such discussion does occur, of course, the language used will be unpredictable for the teacher, and the characteristics of genuine fluency work will accidentally start to appear.

For contrast, below are a number of examples of genuine fluency activity which have been observed in foreign-language classrooms.

The bases for fluency activity

1   The teacher (a Spanish teacher of English in Spain) acts out with one of her students a brief dialogue which she has set up about buying a railway ticket to go to Barcelona. This is done at natural pace, once only. She then tells the class to divide into groups of three and to reconstruct the dialogue. The instruction is given in English, and no further help is offered. The groups, in their second year of English, get out of their seats, divide, and, with great animation, argue about what has happened, much of the argument taking place in English, and construct a dialogue which two members perform, covering more or less the same meaning as the original, but with improvised language, since they cannot possibly remember the form of the English of the original. The teacher goes round the groups, listening and encouraging, and never herself using Spanish. At the end of the lesson, with much laughter, several versions are shown to the rest of the class, all of them in reasonable English, and none very far from the meaning of the original, about which there had been much argument in the groups.

2   A class of Croatian children, in groups of four, struggle to produce the best possible answers to comprehension questions on a passage in their English textbook. The questions are not designed for group discussion, but there is still a lot to do, even though the answers are fairly straightforward, for their English is weak, and they rely heavily on relevant quotation from the passage, which is in front of them, and a limited range of discussion strategies which they have picked up from the teacher's language when he joins the group. He is a Croatian.

3   A mixed-language group of adults in London plans and executes a complicated role-play in which they have to adopt specified roles and personalities provided for them on cards. These involve the drivers, witnesses, and the police at a collision between two cars. The language is entirely that improvised, and polished co-operatively by the students, though they are heavily constrained by the specified situation and characters. However, the management talk that accompanies the preparation affords genuine fluency practice.

4   A second-language class in Africa discusses a work of African literature in small groups. Each group has been asked to isolate the most important event in a specified chapter of the novel, and to argue about why they think it important for the rest of the book. Later in the lesson the groups come together (one group has been working on each chapter) and give their agreed decisions to the teacher, who writes them on the blackboard. A full class discussion follows, in which representatives of different groups argue about whether they agree with the suggestions of other groups. Gradually, links are built up between events in different chapters, and a scheme of the relationships between different events in the book is sketched on the blackboard. The teacher acts simply as intermediary and clarifier of points: the final scheme derives from the discussion, not from a preconceived model, though unfruitful connections may have been discouraged by the identification of particularly sensitive or skilled readers from the class to argue against them.

5 An American teacher in Spain mimes a story to the class. She does not
   speak at all, but accepts by gesture any correctly called-out interpretation
   of the story. Almost all the class are participating, calling out suggestions,
   entirely in English, and turning them into contextualised narration when
   asked to. There is a lot of laughter, and a lot of divergent thinking. Not all
   the suggestions are sensible, but all the joking is in English. (This is an
   example of fluency activity with a whole-class structure.)

[Examples of fluency work]

It should be noted that the difference between the types of small-group
activity distinguished in these two sets is not a matter of level of class; it
is much more a matter of the nature of the constraint on divergence. In
fluency activities the only constraints are the capacity of the students and
the demands of the task. In accuracy activities the task will demand a prespecified type of attainment, and no more linguistic freedom will be
accepted.

In terms of our previous discussion, the fluency activities outlined
above will provide opportunities for students to produce and understand
tokens of the language which they may have been made aware of, or even
learnt, during accuracy activities. These activities thus fit in with our
model of the language-teaching process. They also allow, either individually or over a long period, the various characteristics of small groups
which were discussed earlier in this chapter to develop naturally, with or
without manipulation by the teacher. Particularly if groups vary in size
according to the task to be performed, and if they are largely self-
selecting, they will be both supportive and flexible enough to accommodate all but the most antisocial members of a class. This is an important
point, for built into the need for freedom to develop one's own command
of language as best one can is the need not to be pushed into permanent
social relations at the behest of the teacher. Teachers can limit their control of who goes in which group to minor adjustments, unless there are
major problems caused by genuinely antisocial behaviour. The value of
groups for language activity must partly depend on the groups themselves
being seen as natural social groupings, not as compulsory pedagogical
units.

However, there is one weakness in the position that we have outlined
so far, for the examples we have given, for the most part, lack major
intrinsic interest. We seem to have arrived at a position where interactive
techniques can be encouraged in groups, but the student may well expect
a language-learning lifetime of interactive but meaningless activities,
appealing to those who like playing games, but operating in a cognitive
and affective vacuum.[5] Only the literature class (no. 4 of the second set)
and to some extent the comprehension exercise (no. 2 of the second set)

possess the characteristics of serious educational activity as well as genuine interaction.

This could be a major defect, and may even prevent learners from being able to exercise their creative construction capacities. The characteristics of language acquisition discussed in Chapter 2 were the product of a great deal of interaction of various kinds, but it was interaction arising from the necessity to create meanings in a range of different contexts for many different purposes. And the interactive imperative which has been observed in both first- and second-language learners derives from the needs of the learner to benefit from the results of interaction. While there is no doubt that adults can pretend to need things in which they feel no interest in order to obtain language practice, and while many learners will accept the need to simulate as preferable to not using the target language at all, we cannot know the effects of such pretence on the process of language acquisition. In practice, the games and simulations described in 1 and 3 of the fluency activities above have a role to play, but it cannot happily be a major role in a long-term language programme. Such techniques are frequently used with great success in short courses for intermediate and advanced adults or adolescents – but these are building on the basic work, however inadequate it may appear to be, of earlier teachers in more conventional schools. The dialogue construction observed in the Spanish school (fluency activity 1 above) was only a small part of the total activity in the class, and its excitement depends on the contrast between such an activity and other classroom exercises. While physical activity and creative simulation or role-play will always have useful contributions to make, they cannot in themselves constitute a basis for a long-term developmental strategy for developing fluency. We cannot think of group-work activity simply as a series of techniques without losing the cognitive and intellectual dimension which becomes increasingly important in education as learners mature, and which is a major motivating force for adult learners. More important, though, we cannot ignore this dimension without castrating the language being produced, and returning it to the position of being mere display. The kind of dynamic, but empty interaction produced by simulation exercises runs the risk of displaying functional behaviour as unrealistically as structural exercises display grammatical behaviour. For this reason, we shall have to turn, in the next chapter, to the issue of syllabus organisation and development. This will not be an easy area to examine, for the requirements of a syllabus based on unpredictable language will be quite different from those for the accuracy part of the work, where the language is teacher-determined, and specifiable.

5.4 Fluency in comprehension

The second communicative ability that we isolated at the beginning of this chapter was comprehension. In fact, both of the remaining two major abilities to be developed in school have in the past been based on fluency to a much greater extent than conversation has. Comprehension, in particular, since it is a hidden operation, has been less subject to teacher intervention than either speech or writing. Every time the teacher tells a story to a class, or presents any extended speech which is both accessible and worth listening to in its own right, and every time students are expected to read an appropriate extended text for its content, they are engaged in fluency activities. But here as elsewhere it is possible, of course, for the teacher to insist on testing the results of the reading or listening, so that the exercise becomes one of anticipating what is to be tested, rather than the development of any kind of interaction with the language that the student is interested in pursuing.

The basis of the model of language teaching that we have presented here is the disjuncture between teacher input and learner use. There is, in comprehension, a role for specific, accuracy-based work, and this may take the form of intensive reading exercises of various kinds, of aural comprehension work, even of translation. Students may need to expand their awareness of specific items of vocabulary, structure, or phonology, and of discourse conventions in written or spoken texts; they may need to be made aware of the existence and use of special effects in the language – metaphorical convention, cultural reference, orthographic or phonological deviations from the norm; they will need to have experience of processing language in chunks, and of relating the meanings they encounter to their own cultural presuppositions, without imposing their expectations on messages based on different presuppositions. All of these activities can be assisted by specific work, in which questions provided by the teacher or textbook guide students to become aware of features of the language or message.[6] As we saw in the Croatian example (fluency activity 2 above), such exercises may also provide the occasion for fluency conversation. But the reading that was carried out prior to the discussion, whether it was done co-operatively or individually, cannot be considered fluency reading, for the choice of text did not lie with the student – whether to break off or continue was dependent on the teacher – and above all, the objective of the activity was not to understand such parts of the text as were of interest to the student's preoccupations, but to provide a preparation for analytical activity prompted by the questions which were discussed later by the class. Two major kinds of activity beyond this would be necessary for the establishment of fluency reading in school.

The first way of establishing a fluency basis for reading is to have in operation genuine class libraries, accompanied by encouragement, but not compulsion, to read. Such libraries are, of course, heavily dependent on administrative support for stocking and organisation (see Bright and McGregor, 1970: 65–8; and Broughton *et al.*, 1978: 110–14, for discussion of ways of organising extensive reading). Although some sort of feedback mechanism – book report forms, perhaps – is often enjoyed by students, any more developed testing apparatus will conflict with the fluency aims. The books need to be graded for length, subject matter, and linguistic level only to the minimum extent necessary to make them accessible to the learners. The essential feature of a class library is that it should result in a large quantity of reading. The quality cannot be evaluated without destroying the process, and must be left for the part of the programme devoted to intensive reading. Consequently, the key factors are the quantity and attractiveness of material available, combined with the administrative arrangements for ensuring rapid and efficient exchange of books. Creation of reading habits will depend partly on the general climate in the class, partly on the capacities that have been developed in the formal language work, and partly on the availability of appropriate material. The actual performance of fluent reading may take place in class, where there is a large-scale commitment to English – for example, where there are eight lessons a week one may easily be committed entirely to silent reading – or at home; but there are definite advantages in having some fluency reading performed in class, for it gives the activity status, which it may otherwise lack, and creates a disciplined atmosphere in which initial difficulties may be overcome. However much of the *basis* for reading abilities may derive from active discussion work, in the last resort this must be an activity performed in relative isolation, in concentrated interaction with a text on one's own.

But this is not the only kind of activity which contributes to fluent reading. Any kind of project work which requires students to make use of texts in the target language – skimming, reading for specific information, consulting, reading and extracting ideas – integrates fluency reading into the larger goals of the project. Consequently, suitably graded reference works will also be a prerequisite for the development of the fluency part of a comprehension programme. However, it is difficult to see in principle any other form of organising base for fluency work in reading. We are faced with a choice of either free access to a range of texts, or a limited access to texts which will be used according to the requirements of a larger objective, as part of a programme on a larger scale. An example of this latter type would be a continuing project in which students in groups are expected to produce a recorded radio programme about their country, in the target language. Different groups are allocated specific topics – religion, transport, the economy, ethnic groups, education, sport, the arts, etc. – and are expected to write a script and rehearse the presentation over a long period, perhaps six weeks. Much of the activity associated with this integrated project will be fluency discussion, coupled with more or less fluent writing, but the initial search for appropriate material may be based on reading of relevant source information. Insofar as the reading is the same kind of reading as would be performed in the mother tongue with the same kind of exercise, this will be fluency reading.

Fluency listening is rarer in class as a formal activity, though teachers do sometimes read and tell stories in second languages. The ideal, probably, would be for a teacher to include a short spell of narration – a joke, a story, an anecdote – from the very beginning of the course as a component of every lesson. However, there are problems about establishing a routine in which students are trying too hard to understand. The best fluency listening will probably be peripheral: the instructions through which the teacher organises the class, the casual remarks which accompany teaching points but which are not being focused on. Such talk will be a necessary side-product of the teacher's personal relationship with the class, and may be very difficult to plan for or to generalise about. There are also, of course, opportunities for fluency listening at more advanced levels in cassette and film materials which are specifically prepared for extended listening activities, so long as there is no formal follow-up based on the language items being listened to. It is probable too, that certain formal devices, like songs and recitations of poetry which have persisted in foreign-language teaching even after they have been widely criticised, may constitute fluency listening practice through sheer repetition, and have a value if appropriately graded to the level of the users. Certainly, regular linguistic routines have a place in mother-tongue language acquisition, and in the work of many teachers of foreign languages.

5.5 Fluency in writing

Writing poses a problem for fluency activity which is not posed by any of the other basic abilities. We seem to monitor our writing, as native speakers, rather more consciously than we monitor our speech, and by its stability writing is available for revision, both by the author and by others. Further, writing, because it cannot be adjusted in response to the apparent incomprehension of the interlocutor, requires a more rigidly idealised linguistic patterning. Thus, whether we are dealing with native speakers or non-native speakers, 'errors' are unacceptable. If we couple this with the fact that writing has a major ideological role in literate societies as a means of establishing who has access to what kinds of knowledge (Stubbs, 1980: 29–32), we can see that the writing of the beginner non-native users of the language will often be both incomprehensible and heavily marked as uneducated, whether or not the writers are uneducated in their mother-tongue cultures. When we write, the text becomes public as an artefact independent of the writer, and is judged therefore by socially decontextualised criteria.

The most frequent solution to this problem has been to concentrate the attention of teachers and students almost exclusively on accuracy work at the early stages of writing. Even after problems of the script have been overcome – as they have to be for many learners – writing is usually conceived of as the construction of written sentences, or of controlled paragraphs, with little or no linguistic freedom and no content freedom being offered to the writer (Dykstra, Port, and Port, 1968; Jupp and Milne, 1968; Alexander, 1971; etc.). It is generally held that learners should first master the language system in a mechanical way, and only then hope to branch out on their own.

Controlled writing exercises may be regarded as a monolingual attempt to perform a similar function to that of translation into the target language in grammar–translation approaches. But whereas translation did often demand that texts of some intrinsic interest might be used, however inappropriately, controlled and guided composition seems invariably to produce texts which are totally trivial. It is unfair to blame the writers of textbooks for this, for the rules of the exercise demand an attention to form which would be destroyed if the learner became too interested in content. Nonetheless, the gap between the creativity of young writers in mother tongue and the activities of second-language learners is very striking, and we need to ask whether there is not a role for genuine writing, even if accompanied by formal incompetence, in the second-language classroom.

One attempted solution has already been referred to in 4.1, where a Manichaean strategy was adopted, with one part of the course consisting of a highly rigid series of controlled and guided writing exercises, and another encouraging totally free writing which would be discussed only in terms of its ideas and content, with no reference to formal errors except where they impeded communication. It is significant that teachers who have been exposed to the distinction between accuracy and fluency have been least happy with it in this form, applied to writing, and there may indeed be arguments for allowing students to write their own ideas and to produce corrected forms with guidance from the teacher.

It is also possible to create the conditions for group revision and improvement of written work, so that the accuracy activity is turned into something of a conscious but relatively spontaneous exercise, for talking *about* accuracy may be fluency talk. But at some point writers will need to integrate their thinking to the process of creating written language. Traditional free writing activities for advanced students have always performed this function (though it is important to note that much native-speaker writing is situational and semi-guided, as with journalists or university students, rather than free and creative), and there are opportunities for creative and situational writing in such activities as the radio-programme project described in 5.4 above. Whether we can do more than provide some degree of stimulation for creative writing, through class magazines and projects, and couple this with more controlled work when necessary, is an open question. It is not a question which has been answered, or even addressed, by the standard texts on the teaching of writing (Byrne, 1979; White, 1980).

5.6 A 'natural' linguistic environment

We have seen that the use of pair and group work is the only available basis for naturalistic behaviour in conversational interaction in class, and that work on this basis can increase the amount and intensity of practice during oral work. We have also seen that the same mode of class organis-ation can create a context for activity in accuracy work for reading and writing. However, in the last resort, both of these activities must be isolated linguistic patterns of behaviour, and the use of groups, for correc-tion of written work or for preparation for reading, must be seen as a pedagogic device which should not dominate the need to leave students alone to get on with their own work. The use of groups may help to create an appropriate atmosphere for independent work, but it cannot substi-tute for the necessary training of students to operate entirely on their own in reading or writing. Consequently, the prime value of group work lies in its ability to stimulate natural language activity in discussion and conversation.

But natural language use, for most people, is primarily discussion and conversation. Reading and writing may well develop out of a secure foun-dation of linguistic interaction, and a classroom dominated by the literate abilities may be less efficient as a language-learning environment than one in which the reading and writing arise out of a genuine language-using community, even if the language being genuinely used is an interlanguage or a pidgin. But this observation raises major problems which we shall address later.

6 The 'content' of language teaching: language and meaning

We have seen that it is possible to place students in classroom groups which will make more or less natural interaction possible through the medium of the target language, and we have noted that students will also require opportunities for individual work in order to master reading and writing. In principle, then, it is possible for the classroom to provide for the same kinds of social relations that language learners encounter when they have the benefit of immersion. There remain, however, two other major issues to examine. The first is the relationship between classroom language and meaning, and the second the problem of making up for the rich linguistic data available to the natural learner but normally unavailable to the classroom learner. In this chapter we shall be examining ways of making the language of the classroom meaningful.

6.1 Process and product

Language teaching has no obvious content in the sense that history or physics teaching may be said to have. Indeed, the term 'content' is frequently ambiguous in discussions of language teaching, for it can refer simultaneously to the items of language that may be selected for the syllabus or curriculum design, or to the topics which may be included in reading, writing, or speaking – the subject matter of linguistic interactions. We shall start here by considering the problem of items of language, and move on to look at content as subject matter of messages.

Before we look at the problems of syllabus specification, however, it is worth noting that the climate of educational opinion has changed, in the last twenty years, in its attitude to 'content' subjects, and there is a great deal more emphasis now than in the past on all subjects as essentially 'process' subjects (Parker and Rubin, 1966). The key text in this development was probably Bruner's *The Process of Education* (Bruner, 1960) with its insistence that

What a scientist does at his desk, or in the laboratory, what a literary critic does in reading a poem are of the same order as what anybody does when he is engaged in like activities – if he is to achieve understanding. The difference is in degree, not in kind. The schoolboy learning physics *is* a physicist, and it is easier for him to learn physics behaving like a physicist than doing something else.

(Bruner, 1960: 14)

If we substitute 'language user' for 'physicist' in the last sentence, we shall arrive at a position consistent with the argument of this study. However, this is not the reason for citing Bruner at this point. He is primarily concerned that the underlying *concepts* of traditional disciplines, the basic systems of thought, should be taught in school, particularly as such facts in those disciplines as are taught are only valuable for their significance in the systems of thought which constitute 'thinking as a physicist' (or a historian, botanist, or whatever). The humanistic movement, discussed in 5.2 above, developed partly in response to what was perceived to be an excessive intellectualisation in Bruner's ideas (R.M. Jones, 1968), but the insistence of humanistic educators on a holistic view of the learning process was implicit in Bruner's view of 'being a physicist' rather than simply 'knowing facts about physics'.

But this shift in direction in education generally does not make content subjects the same as skill subjects like language, although it does allow some convergence of interest. With reference to the traditional goals of education, as they relate to goals for human life (to improve our understanding of our condition and of the world, to create beauty, to live morally), language learning can only have a facilitating role, whereas most other subject areas relate directly to these goals. But if language learning facilitates activity towards these goals, there is at least a possibility that school language learning could be more closely related to some of the objectives it is intended to facilitate.

It may perhaps be worthwhile to start our discussion by looking at some of the changes in education which reflect contemporary concerns. Summarising a symposium on 'Facts and feelings in the classroom', Rubin (1973) asks for nine major changes:

1 We must shift the basis of the curriculum from an arbitrary selection of subject matter to that which is of immediate importance to the child's development.
2 We must seek to deal with feelings as well as facts, fashioning a curriculum that provides a better balance between cognition and affect.
3 We must seek to build the child's inner strengths as we attempt to improve his emotional response to the world.
4 We must look anew for content of greater significance: for learning experiences that have a stronger connection with the child's external world and for educational processes that integrate knowledge, feeling, and behaviour.
5 We must begin to invent a repertory of instructional procedures that make it possible for children of different bents to achieve the same educational gains.
6 We must alter the environment of the school so that it becomes a more rewarding place in which to be.
7 We must look discerningly at our rapidly changing society and anticipate, as best we can, the knowledge that will be of the most worth in the time ahead.
8 We must grant our young the right to formulate the values by which they wish to live.
9 We must operate different kinds of schools, designed for different educational

purposes, allowing individuals to pursue their own special needs and prefer-
ences.

(Rubin, 1973: 261–2)

These demands are both very grand and very vague, but they are typical of a tendency which has rejected the isolation of intellectual learning from other aspects of development. Contemporary discussion of language teaching has been responsive to many of these demands. The first, for example, may be related to the development of needs analyses (Richterich, 1972; Munby, 1978), the second and third to the depth-psychology approach of Stevick (1976), and the fifth to the widespread discussion of individualisation (Altman and Politzer, 1971; Altman and James, 1980). However, contemporary syllabus design still follows fairly closely the model of Taba (1962: 12), in which seven steps are taken in order:

1 needs analysis;
2 formulation of objectives;
3 selection of content;
4 organization of content;
5 selection of learning activities;
6 organization of learning activities;
7 decisions about what needs evaluating and how to evaluate.

This model makes sense if we are choosing an agreed body of knowledge to be presented to a predictable group of learners, but even for content subjects it has been attacked as unnecessarily restrictive (Parker and Rubin, 1966: 17–21). They raise a number of objections, but for our purposes the most important is their contention that

Facts, principles, laws and concepts are one kind of content; the processes in which they can be used are another; the methods by which these are learned are still another kind of content.

(Parker and Rubin, 1966: 21)

Particularly when we are dealing with a facilitating subject like language, the processes of classroom methodology may usefully be considered part of the content; for it is only through what students are being asked to do with the language in the classroom that they will be exposed (at least in foreign-language learning) to a model of the possible uses of language. Yet frequently the language is taught as a code (even a code for use) without the potential activity – what it is to be a 'French/Chinese/Arab speaker of English' – being systematically thought out at all. If language is primarily facilitative, language-teaching methodology should activate the facilitative function with reference to something worth facilitating. This complaint takes us well beyond the capacities of conventional needs analysis, for needs analysis has operated passively as a sociolinguistic tool, without relating itself to the moral, intellectual, or aesthetic needs which were referred to earlier. The teaching of general English, or French, or any other language cannot be 'directly derivable from the prior identification of the communication needs of that particular participant or participant stereotype' (Munby, 1978: 218) except when learners have prestatable and stable needs. Yet stability and predictability in human interaction is precisely what schools have an interest in preventing, if innovation, imagination, and creativity are desired products of schooling. In the ESP context which Munby has defined, the presumptions of his and similar models will have value; but for more general purposes, a specification of communicative competence, directly applied, will have exactly the same risks as a specification of linguistic competence directly applied. It will isolate the means from the ends, so that only those who are specifically interested in the acquisition of linguistic systems as ends in themselves – a small minority – will benefit by intrinsic motivation. We should be interested in a capacity to perform creatively, not in a limitation of creativity by prior specification.

But there is a more directly linguistic version of the 'process as content' argument to be considered. While we cannot but admit that many language learners have learnt foreign languages successfully using highly mechanical procedures (Pickett, 1978), the interpretation of such evidence is by no means simple. Insofar as such learners can be classified as good language users, they have clearly had experience of language use (and if they could not be so classified we would not accept them as evidence for successful language learning). It is probably true that such learners are particularly skilled accuracy learners, in terms of our model, but the integration of the system that they have built up accurately into fluency activity has clearly happened at some point for them, even if they claim to have mastered the language system before attempting to use it. But other learners in the same survey, and the learners examined in Naiman, Fröhlich, Stern, and Todesco, 1978, exhibit fairly consistent tendencies, which are summarised as follows:

1 The learner must be active in his approach to learning and practice;
2 The learner must come to grips with the language as a system;
3 The learner must use the language in real communication;
4 The learner must monitor his interlanguage;
5 The learner must come to terms with the affective demands of language learning.

(Naiman, Fröhlich, Stern, and Todesco, 1978: 103)

These observations, which are based both on schoolchildren in the classroom and on successful adult learners, provide us with a useful starting point for examining the 'process as content' in language teaching.

An acceptance of the methodological principles examined in Chapters 3, 4 and 5, will already have carried us much of the way towards a recognition of the language acquisition process as part of the language course. But we still have to look at ways of organising the language items which will occur as part of the accuracy teaching, and at some of the syllabus design proposals which have implications for fluency activity. Although it would be possible to identify 'accuracy' with 'product', and 'fluency' with 'process', a clear separation between the two, such as we have envisaged, would obviously not answer the criticisms of those who call for an integration. How, then, can our model operate within a syllabus?

6.2 Proposals for 'communicative' content

Corder (1973: 322) concludes a discussion of principles of syllabus design with a warning that 'there is no such thing as a perfect, ideal or logical syllabus . . . Ideally, each learner requires a "personalised" syllabus of his own. But we teach groups, not individuals. Any syllabus is bound, therefore, to be something of a compromise.' But we have seen that it is unsatisfactory in principle to separate the learning of a language from the social use of a language, and any use of language is a compromise. It is specifically within the process of compromising with the demands and strategies of other language users that language acquisition occurs. Perhaps, therefore, if we can find an appropriate way of *compromising*, we shall benefit the learner more than if we try to identify the in-built syllabus of a learner operating in isolation.

But it is isolated syllabuses that constitute the main body of traditional language syllabuses – isolated in the sense that they assume that language learning will be carried out by individuals requiring a specified body of content. Corder comments (p. 322) that 'what we finish up with is some sort of integrated but parallel set of syllabuses: syntactic, phonological, cultural and functional and within each of these a parallel set of learning tasks', and others have made the same point with even larger lists. Swan (1981: 39), for example, includes Corder's four syllabuses, but adds lexical, notional, topic, situational, discourse, rhetorical, and stylistic syllabuses as well. There is in fact some confusion here, for the various types of syllabus can be related to one another more systematically than Swan implies ('discourse', 'rhetoric', and 'style', as he defines them, are three different ways of looking at the same phenomenon), but they are all based on analytical categories from the point of view of the observer of language activity.

Behavioural objectives

Surveying the early development of communicative syllabuses, Shaw (1977) points to the shift away from specification of language content towards a concern for behavioural objectives. The possible options for a behaviourally sensitive syllabus are seen as 'situational', 'thematic' and 'notional' or 'functional'. Wilkins (1976: 17) criticises situational syllabuses on the grounds that language which occurs in a given situation is never absolutely predictable, as it will be dependent on the speakers' intentions, and elsewhere (1972: 83–4) points out the difficulties inherent in defining 'situation' and in enabling learners to generalise from language encountered in one situation to the demands of another. Similar criticisms may be made of the generalisability of functional syllabuses (Widdowson, 1978c: 35), and Shaw himself (1977: 222) does not see the topic approach as applicable to normal language-teaching situations because the language items will occur (except, no doubt, for some lexis) in a haphazard fashion. We shall examine this issue in more detail when we consider the Bangalore Project.

The problem with all the approaches mentioned so far is that they ignore Bruner's concern with the characteristic system of the subject being taught. Topical or situational activity may provide a convenient basis for teaching, but the convenience is administrative: it does not emerge out of the essential nature of language itself. And although functional activity corresponds more closely to our understanding of the essential characteristics of language, it is open to similar objections to those raised against situational organisation, for we cannot predict in advance all the possible functions to which users may wish to put their language – these are in principle infinite. Unless we can produce a relatively finite set of rules for functioning with a given language, and demonstrate that such rules are not largely available to learners through their knowledge of how to operate in their mother tongues, there is little argument for building up a syllabus of functions. A syllabus which consists of unrelatable because unsystematisable items can be no more than a checklist. We shall argue in a moment that there is value in a checklist, but it should be as a substitute for a syllabus only if there is no alternative means of systematisation. The only remaining category from Shaw's list is Wilkins' 'notional', in its non-functional realisations as 'semantico-grammatical categories'. But it is difficult to see how these can be realised in syllabus design without either relating them to structural syllabuses (where such categories appeared often in the later stages – as 'result', 'purpose', 'concession', etc.), or to arbitrarily selected topics or situations, with the vulnerability to the objections already raised.

The difficulty is that a language user is not someone who becomes aware of the structure of language in the sense that a physicist will become aware of the structure of matter: becoming a language user is not becoming a linguist. But at the same time the attempt to understand the structure of language which characterises the linguist is an attempt to create a tidy system by which to account for the diverse phenomena which characterise human linguistic behaviour. But insofar as we wish to make our language teaching coherent to either learners or teachers, we have little choice but to turn to the systems of linguists. The crucial question is whether we want to make our language teaching coherent in terms of the product, as linguists do, or whether we can rely on an unspecifiable process, or whether we want to combine the two.

In a more recent survey of approaches to second-language syllabuses, Crawford-Lange (1982) has distinguished systems-behavioural designs from problem-posing ones. The former type is dependent on an analysis of the subject matter into discrete learning units to be mastered; the latter 'puts culture in the *central* position and understands language as a communicative tool expressive of that culture' (p. 88). The language is subordinated to a desire to examine matters of interest to students, in response to the ideas of Freire (1971; 1981). This may appear to be a promising approach from the point of view of this study, but it is important to note the warning that there has been no serious evaluation or examination of such procedures (Crawford-Lange, 1982: 91) in second-language teaching, though they remain suggestive for our purposes, and will be returned to when we discuss problem-solving approaches.

In principle, any systematic analysis of language or language behaviour could be turned into discrete learning units and thus fit into a systems-behavioural design, so functional–notional syllabuses could be treated as a sub-class of that design. Certainly, much language-learning material allegedly based on such principles appears to resemble mastery-learning material (Andrews, 1975; L. Jones, 1977). Crawford-Lange groups functional–notional syllabuses with a range of interdisciplinary approaches, however, as different ways of organising *content*. The latter include relating language teaching to work in other subjects in the curriculum, career-based language teaching (for example, French for secretarial careers) and language as part of social science. Finally, the survey examines four different 'instructional alternatives': the three so-called 'humanistic' methods of Counselling Learning, Suggestopaedia, and The Silent Way, and Co-operative Learning, based on Johnson and Johnson, 1975, which is essentially a procedure based on small-group co-operation.

A model for content specification

It does not seem to be helpful, though, for Crawford-Lange to equate language content with subject matter. Nor should we allow the claim that 'process is content' simply to be an excuse for grouping all aspects of language teaching together without any regard for important conceptual distinctions. The approaches examined seem to have three general categories of analysis for the linguistic product, corresponding approximately to form, meaning, and use. The categories for form generally derive from descriptive linguistics, those for use from social psychology, philosophy, anthropology, and stylistics, and those for meaning from whatever field is the subject of discussion. The process choices which the survey discusses, however, seem to be limited to packages of various kinds produced as language-teaching methods, and they will require more precise analysis than they have received. The various possibilities for a more rigorous analysis are summarised in the following table, and glossed in the succeeding pages.

1 *Analysis of product*

   a) Formal analyses
      (linguists' categories):

                                  phonological
                                  syntactic
                                  morphological
                                  notional (semantico-
                                  grammatical)

   b) Interactional analyses
      (social psychologists',
      anthropologists', and
      stylisticians' categories):   situational
                                  functional
              leading to:
                                  discoursal, rhetorical, and
                                  stylistic

   c) Content/topical analyses
      (technical or general
      categories):   i) socially directed:
                                cultural

                     ii) educationally directed:
                                interdisciplinary

                   iii) language directed:
                                linguistics
                                literature

2 *Analysis of process*

   a) Communicative abilities
      (see discussion, p. 69):   conversation/discussion
                                  comprehension
                                  extended writing
                                  (extended speaking)[1]

   b) Orientation
      (see discussion, pp. 52–7):   accuracy
                                  fluency

c) Pedagogical mode
   (see discussion below):

individual
private interactional (pairs
   or small groups)
public interactional (whole
   class / large groups + teacher)

[*Types of content specification*]

If our objectives are communicative performance, then our classroom processes will always be directed towards one of the four groups of abilities discussed on page 69. However, the orientation of an activity in class may be towards either accuracy or fluency at any given moment, and in accuracy work the pedagogical mode adopted will not automatically be dictated by the nature of the final interaction being aimed at. There may sometimes, for example, be private preparation for participation in conversation (learners may need time to think about what they are going to say, and this is not normally a feature of casual conversation, but it has pedagogical value in allowing learners to enter a conversation with reasonably accurate predictions of what may occur). There may also be small-group activity as part of intensive reading work, though the communicative objective is individual silent reading. A third example is public discussion of the preparation for individual writing, in which the teacher establishes a general plan with the whole class, and calls upon individuals to make public suggestions.

We thus have three major categories for the analysis of process: one concerned with the ultimate objective in language use; one with the orientation of the student towards language use or towards monitoring; and one concerned with the mode of classroom activity. There seems to be little justification for classifying the pedagogical mode more finely, for the three categories of individual, private, and public exhaust the interactional possibilities, being respectively independent, equal, and unequal in social relations. Since the emphasis in all our discussion has been on opportunities for self-creation of linguistic environment and self-development of dialect, a rigid specification of the process of interaction in terms such as those prompted by 1(b) would defeat the objective of the teaching procedure, and would turn a process category into a product one. It would of course be possible, if this were a scheme for the analysis of classroom behaviour, to specify the kinds of exercises that are performed as accuracy activities (cf. Mitchell, Parkinson, and Johnstone, 1981), and the exact nature of the teacher involvement. But insofar as accuracy activity relates to product, analyses in section 1 will contribute to the specification of exercise types, and it is not the intention of this table to produce an exhaustive list so much as one which accounts for the unavoidable features of a communicative methodology, as defined in this study. We can claim, therefore, that the list of communicative abilities exhausts the possibilities, that the binary choice on orientation is decisive, for reasons which have been discussed, and that the social context of teaching is limited to the three categories of pedagogical mode. Within each of these there will be an infinite number of possible activities, though in practice the teacher's choice will be limited by conventional expectations, and all these choices will be capable of being analysed in terms of all the dimensions of product analysis listed under section 1. Activities may also, of course, be focused primarily on only one dimension, especially for the purpose of correction of observed deficiencies – for example, minimal-pair drills.

It is suggested that an analysis of process along the lines of section 2 will be far more valuable than reference to particular 'methods', for – as Rivers points out (1980) – the various 'new methods' share general characteristics with good teaching practice anywhere. The appropriate level of generality for an analysis which is intended to improve teaching must be one which can be interpreted by teachers in any circumstances and leave them free to translate general principles into specific, locally sensitive practice. Only thus will the Popperian principles of feedback and adaptation be able to operate.

Two further comments need to be made about the types of content specification, this time with reference to section 1. The bases of all except (c) (iii) were discussed earlier in this chapter. However, it has often been claimed that some self-consciousness about language – even elementary linguistics – is an important part of the language syllabus (for a recent example of this claim, see Ullman, 1981), and it is also frequently claimed that literature has an important role to play in developing linguistic ability, even in the foreign language. Both of these may be claimed as language-directed content, therefore, while the interdisciplinary demands for work within the general curriculum of the school, and the cultural demands as part of the social sensitivity necessary for operating in a target culture, define themselves as the two other significant categories.

Finally, there is one significant, but deliberate omission. No lexical specification is listed. This is because lexical choices, if they are to be principled, will arise out of the other categories. Morphological, syntactic, and notional criteria, as well as situational, functional, and content criteria, will always have a major effect on selection of lexis. In fact it is impossible to conceive of a selection of lexical items which is based on criteria that have no explicit interaction either with meaning, form, or function – unless we imagine a random working through either a dictionary or a thesaurus. Consequently, whereas checklists of items in all the other analyses will have value in defining the appropriate range of particular sets of materials and syllabus specifications, the lexicon can be regarded as potentially always present, to be called upon, as a dictionary is by adults, whenever there is a need in terms of one of the other items. Lexical items which are not justified in terms of other specification will be impossible to integrate with the learner's developing language, and consequently will be disfunctional.

Systematicity

We have, then, a number of ways of specifying the language which is produced by the learners, or the language to which they are exposed. The important question for us is the extent to which analysts' categories of the kinds indicated in section 1 are appropriate for the task of developing effective language performance by learners – that is, the extent to which they will lead teachers to promote effective performance.

There is no doubt that all of these potential taxonomies could be useful as checklists. They could be used *after* the event as ways of ensuring adequate coverage of items which may not have occurred in the process of interaction between teacher and class. Their usefulness as a prior basis for syllabus design, however, will depend on the ease with which they can be made accessible to learners in a form compatible with learning theory, for a syllabus presupposes a design which specifically facilitates learning, not simply a random joining together of elements with no particular cohesion or system. To demand systematicity for a syllabus does not automatically command assent (Wilkins, Brumfit, and Paulston, 1981), but the arguments in favour of systematicity are compelling. Whatever else we may not know about learning, we do know that what can be made systematic by the learner is more likely to be learnt than random elements, so – even if the system arrived at in describing language is not in fact the system that learners operate with – we should not discard, without strong reasons, what can be made systematic for what cannot. At the present state of our understanding, the categories of formal analyses, and of content analyses (1(a) and (c) in our chart), may be capable of systematisation, but there is little possibility of systematising situational or functional categories. The most sophisticated attempt to do this for functions, Halliday's work (1973; 1978), relates functional demands to formal structures, but only within a limited framework, and for our purposes this could be regarded as an extension of the syntactic system.

We seem to have a choice, then, between the more or less traditional formal linguistic categories, or the systematisation imposed by content, in disciplines such as linguistics, cultural analysis, or other subjects, as in immersion programmes. What are the most important criteria for making our choice? There seem to be four possibilities: we can insist on one or other of these types of system; we can insist that both types are necessary;

or we can reject the claims of either, arguing that language differs from other types of learning and does not require systematicity.

The demand for a systematic exposure to the language, defined in formal terms, is widespread, and is perhaps implicit in no. 2 of the characteristics of the good language learner, cited earlier, at the end of 6.1. It can also be found in the 'humanistic' methodologies (see Gattegno, 1972: 34–50). The demand for another kind of system based on content is less often stated explicitly, though Widdowson and Brumfit (1981) claim that a true notional syllabus can be developed through the increasing conceptual demands of a discipline; Widdowson (1968; 1978b) has proposed teaching other subjects through English for other reasons; and the immersion programmes of Canada – now being experimented with in the USA (P.A. Hornby, 1980), and the Soviet Union (Bartley, 1971: 22–30) – clearly share similar assumptions.

There is, of course, no reason why an institution should not combine both types of syllabus, and in fact this seems to be what happens in Soviet special language schools (Bartley, 1971, chap. III), where the role of the specific language classes seems to correspond approximately to our 'accuracy', and the teaching of subjects such as geography in the target language corresponds to our 'fluency'. It is perhaps surprising that I have been unable to locate any fully integrated courses in which a graded language programme is associated closely with the development of subject matter, except in African primary schools (McAdam, 1970), for an entirely integrated version of linguistic and content syllabuses might seem to represent the safest course, at least in second-language situations.

The argument that neither type of system is necessary for formal language teaching underlies the strong argument for functional syllabuses. Wilkins agrees that language may be specified, but rejects the idea of a language-based system as a source:

... since it is language behaviour we are concerned with, it is possible, indeed desirable, that the linguistic content of any unit should also be stated, but it is a content that is derived from the initial behavioural analysis.

(Wilkins, 1976: 13)

Without an indication of the nature of a behavioural system, this amounts to a rejection of system altogether. However, as Wilkins does not discuss learning theory, it is unclear to what extent this is a conscious rejection. For Lozanov, in contrast, the rejection is specific and is related to his view of the peripheral nature of learning. Referring to recordings for students who have spare time for study, he writes:

The important thing is that these recordings are not the conventional type of exercises for the repetition of lessons and for memorizing lexical and grammatical elements. They must be whole meaningful texts (not of a fragmentary nature) and, above all, interesting. It is important that no analysis and no translation of all the different elements of these recordings are made. They must be listened to for the sake of the music of the foreign speech. The meaning of the speech should be left to surface in the minds of the students, by itself, without stress and without any unpleasant efforts.

(Lozanov, 1978: 277)

However, this refusal to emphasize the conscious assault on the language system is accompanied by a psychological justification:

The material must be presented in meaningful aggregates, and must be communicative. The textbook should have motivational force, and should be entertaining and interesting to the students. Its psychological structure should be given prominence and stressed, while the language problems must be 'smuggled' in unobtrusively without alarming and worrying the students.

(Lozanov, 1978: 278)

This demand arises out of the claim that language is best memorised when the learner is exposed to suggestion rather than to an overt and self-conscious presentation of the system. But there are major doubts about the reliability and validity of the evidence presented by Lozanov (Scovell, 1979),[2] and he is referred to here simply to illustrate the possibility of rejecting language system if a learning theory can support such a view. The problem with work on suggestology is that it is concerned almost exclusively with the process of memorisation, and neglects the needs of long-term construction and improvisation of linguistic systems.

Whichever choice we make among these alternatives, it must surely be dependent on our view of language learning. It is certainly clear, as our discussion in Chapter 2 showed, that native speakers and foreign learners can, when immersed in the language, acquire the system without necessarily being made consciously aware of the whole of the system. So we might argue that we can do without systematic exposure to the target language when we have immersion, as in second-language situations, or when we can create the conditions of immersion in the classroom. However, there are two problems. First, not all students who are immersed in a foreign language acquire it with equal ease, and many immigrants never acquire the dominant language. If we are concerned with all students who have to learn a foreign language, we need to provide motivation for learners, and the nature of the syllabus may be an important factor in creating such motivation. The key issue will be the expectations about the nature of learning, or of language learning (they may not be the same), which the students bring to school. The second problem is that, as we saw in Chapter 3, some learners deliberately choose to subject themselves to systematic learning of the structure of the language. Even skilled language learners in an immersion situation may be grateful for access to a formally designed syllabus.

However, it is important that we recognise that a formal design of syllabus can be neutral in its relation to methodology. Whether the formal patterning is presented initially to students (as in a deductive approach) or is revealed after use (as in an inductive approach) or whether it is never formally revealed, but simply provides a structure for a teacher or materials writer to be aware of (as with an audiolingual approach) is not determined by the fact of having a systematic structure. Such decisions are in principle independent of decisions about the design of the syllabus.

We seem, then, to have two different types of information available to us for incorporation in a syllabus: that which is capable of systematisation, and that which is not. From one point of view, only the first can contribute to a syllabus insofar as a syllabus is intended to be a coherent model of what can be learnt. But it probably makes more sense to consider what cannot be systematised as learning material for which we cannot make even a vague prediction of learning processes, while what can be systematised can be hypothetically regarded as a body which will be learnt through its interconnections. We do succeed in learning inchoate collections of material by imposing our own *ad hoc* systematisations.[3] But, for the administrative purposes of syllabus design, the non-systematised material will have to be regarded as a checklist, which can either be taught by means of any perceivable connection that crops up, or which can be regarded as a basis for selection by teachers as and when convenient, without being built into the syllabus in advance. Thus most of the elements in 1(b) of our types of content specification may be added to the linguistic systems, or incorporated in the content systems, whenever appropriate – but there cannot be predictable and absolute decisions about how and where such incorporation should take place.

There is, however, one other possible design for a communicative syllabus which we have not so far examined. This is the syllabus based not on content, nor on language, but on problem-solving operations, each of which exemplifies and generates language, but the grading of which is based on the problems to be solved and not on the language systems themselves. The Bangalore Project provides the most fully developed version of that approach.

6.3   The Bangalore Project

Apart from the series of bulletins from the Regional Institute of English, South India, at Bangalore, the only published report of this project is in Johnson, 1982 (Paper 12, The Procedural Syllabus: 135–44). The discussion here is based on the published sources, my own observations during a visit to the project in March–April 1981, an unpublished paper presented by Dr Prabhu at the TESOL Convention, Honolulu, May 1982, and extensive informal discussion with teachers and organisers of the project, especially Prabhu himself.

The basic assumption of the project is that 'form is best learnt when the learner's attention is on meaning' (Prabhu, 1982: 2). They therefore reject the making of explicit generalisations about the structure of language, any manipulation of the language data in order to facilitate such generalisations, and an incremental syllabus based on linguistic description. This follows from the beliefs that the process of grammar construction by the learner is likely to be a developmental process which is 'organic' rather than 'additive'; that we have no reason to assume that observers' generalisations (whether the observer is a linguist, teacher, or course designer) about language structure correspond to those involved in learners' grammar construction; that such observers' generalisations, being based on 'fully-formed' language competence, will frequently conflict with those that are part of an interlingual grammar; and that consequently any conscious formulation of generalisations is likely to be harmful rather than beneficial as it will distort the learners' own generalisation by imposing inappropriate categories.

Materials have therefore been written which are not based on any overt language syllabus, without any linguistic pre-selection, and without any explicitly language-focused activity. Instead, the materials exploit:

i)   the learner's natural desire to meet a challenge (i.e. to solve a problem to prove that he can do so),
ii) the preoccupation with meaning or thinking which such problem-solving necessarily brings about and
iii) the incidental struggle with language-use which such activity engenders.
(Prabhu, 1982: 3)

We thus have a strong claim, which in many respects resembles that of Lozanov – except that the latter concentrates far more on affective factors in diverting attention from language itself (by means of personae for learners to adopt in the foreign language, attention to the comfort of the classroom, relaxation through music and yoga, and so on) – while Prabhu relies far more heavily on cognitive motivation.

There are, however, important differences between the two sets of projects. The Bangalore Project started in the schools with a dissatisfaction with the structural approach, to which South India had been heavily exposed in the Madras Snowball (D.A. Smith, 1962). The modifications to traditional practice are primarily based on materials, without incorporating widespread change in classroom organisation, technology, or size of class. The extensive testing of materials has been carried out with minimal departure from the normal conditions of school life, with a total of 365 lessons taught in Bangalore to a class of forty girls between 1979–80 and 1981–2, 280 to a class of forty girls in Madras in 1980–1 to 1981–

2, 90 to a class of fifty-five boys in Bangalore in 1981–2, and 125 to a mixed class of thirty in Madras in 1981–2. However, of these four classes, only the last has been taught with problem-solving materials from the very beginning, and as classes approach their final school examinations some modification of the principles becomes necessary in order to accommodate them to the demands of the system. These are, of course, unavoidable difficulties when attempting to innovate in normal school systems. Thus, while it will be extremely difficult to produce an evaluation which will satisfy demands for variable-controlled, psychometrically valid comparisons to be made, the project can claim that it is not trying to make a point about language learning in the abstract, but about language teaching and learning in specific circumstances. However, this is an important project for the purposes of our study, not only because it is addressing itself to a central concern in our argument, but also because it illustrates the kind of study, and the kind of monitoring and publicising, that is necessary if our Popperian principle of sensitive social intervention with maximum opportunities for feedback is to be realised in practice. We shall be making a number of criticisms of the project, but it is important that its significance should not be undervalued. Its value is based on the following considerations:

1 uniquely, it is attempting to evaluate a widely held contemporary hypothesis about language teaching and learning in terms which relate directly to normal teaching situations;

2 methodologically, it provides a rich and realistic basis for informal assessment and evaluation by combining the use of normal classrooms in normal circumstances with provision, through annual seminars and regular circulation of bulletins and newsletters, of constant and public discussion with the interested professional public;

3 it is a locally based experiment, arising directly from a dissatisfaction with existing methods in a concrete situation, and the initiative for the project sprang from a theory-informed concern for improving a specific teaching practice, so that the problems of renewal of connection should be minimised;

4 whether or not the project shows equal or better progress by the experimental groups against the performance of other classes (which are *de facto* control groups), it will have been successful in three important ways:

  a) it will have shown that a careful grass-roots experiment can be executed in the unpropitious circumstances of a poor, third-world education system in which experimentation is closely related to the activation of the teaching profession;

  b) it will have enabled us to obtain valuable evidence about a major current model for language learning, in a non-idealised setting;

  c) it will have developed a set of materials which, with adjustments, can be used as a basis for fluency activities in any language teaching, regardless whether the system is based on the underlying assumptions of Bangalore.

The programme is constructed around a series of problems, requiring the use of English, which have to be solved by the learner. The problems are introduced as specific tasks in which students have to interpret language data – for example, a timetable or set of rules or a map with its rubric – and use the data for particular purposes. Tasks are usually preceded by pre-tasks, in which the teacher performs a task similar to the one that students will be asked to perform themselves, in interaction with the class, using whatever language seems appropriate for this purpose. Thus the level of language used by the teacher is determined by the demands of the problem, and by the teacher's natural powers of simplification, unplanned and spontaneously structured. (Prabhu in conversation makes a great deal of the claim that all language users have a natural capacity to simplify, and that teachers of English are doing what everyone does, not something specifically pedagogic.) During the pre-task, also, some students perform the task, thus providing a guided demonstration of the procedure for solution, and of some language for use by other students. Following the pre-task and the task, there is normally some direct evaluation, in which learners discover whether they have successfully solved the problem, but they receive no intentional evaluation of the English they have produced.

An example of this procedure is as follows (the full text appears in the Appendix, on page 145):

1 A short dialogue is handed to students, and two students read it out loud, each taking a part.
2 Pre-task: the teacher discusses twenty-four free response comprehension questions with the class, asking for answers, and using whatever language comes naturally in order to establish communication.
3 Task: for homework, students are asked to say whether five statements, which are given to them, are true or false with reference to the dialogue. They are asked to give reasons for their choice.
4 The students' true/false answers receive 'marks' so that they are provided with feedback in terms of the task.

                    (Madras girls, lesson 183: 26 August 1981, mimeo)

The tasks have been graded by trial and error, on the assumption that reasonable challenge must be offered, so that the learners have to try quite hard, but that the task should not seem to be impossible. The working rule has been that at least half the class should be successful on at least half the task. There are a number of types of task which recur at different times during the course (for example, interpretations of maps or timetables), and several tasks of the same kind appear in a sequence, each example being slightly more difficult than the previous one.

There is a heavy emphasis on receptive language. Prabhu believes (1982: 4) 'that the development of reception is also the earlier part of the development of production and that learners will produce voluntarily when they are ready for it'. Consequently, compared with the most radical foreign-language classrooms in other countries, these tend to be teacher-centred, though classes recorded and classes observed showed a large amount of apparently spontaneous shouting out, both in response to teacher questions and independently. Perhaps surprisingly, in view of the presuppositions, teachers do correct language produced by students, but primarily for content or clarification of communicative intent. However, they are expected to do this more for writing than in speech. Nor is correctness of language taken into account in evaluation: the sole criterion is the successful performance of the task. When corrections are made, learners are not asked to rewrite (Prabhu, 1982: 5).

The whole programme assumes minimal technology: nothing more is used than blackboard, chalk, paper, and pencil. Only the materials themselves (and some of the teachers who have been teaching in the experimental groups, such as Prabhu himself) are untypical of conventional Indian classrooms.

Prabhu has summarised his defence against two major criticisms, the heavy reliance on reasoning, and the avoidance of group-work procedures (Prabhu, personal communication and 1982: 5). He feels that learners need the security of working with problems in which the answers are clearly right or wrong, and he wishes to encourage guessing and trial-and-error within a reasonably convergent framework, so he prefers a small range of possible answers. He claims that open-ended questions make greater demands on the students' language than is appropriate at this early receptive stage; and he also argues that English is the language of rationality rather than emotion for Indians. It might, however, be objected that the open–closed issue is not strictly the same as the rational–affective one, and – more significantly – that an exclusive reliance on cognitive devices presupposes that learners will be motivated by an essentially intellectual curiosity, which may fail to attract those who are more divergent or artistic (L. Hudson, 1968). However, it is unclear in practice whether Prabhu entirely follows his own precept. Some of the problems demand possible conclusions for exciting folk-tales, and almost all fully contextualised language, such as the dialogue used in illustration above, involves some imaginative identification. The lack of group work is based on a worry that learners will use mother tongue, that it will conflict so firmly with conventions of classroom management that the face validity of the project will suffer, and that learner–learner interaction will promote pidginisation. The last of these is the most significant objection, and will be specifically discussed later, in 8.2.

To some extent the issue of how much interaction in English to encourage is a question which will receive empirical clarification as the project progresses, but it does need to be said that by no means all the students participate overtly (though they may be engaged) in the speaking addressed to the teacher, although those who do often speak with sophistication and apparent spontaneity. It seems likely that group work would have a value, for the educational reasons cited in Chapter 5, even if the linguistic reasons were disagreed with. At the same time, there is increasing evidence in support of a delayed start in production (Postovsky, 1974; Gary, 1978; Gary and Gary, 1982), so that Prabhu may be wise not to force it too early.

There are problems with the Bangalore Project, if it is viewed as a formal experiment. In spite of the dissemination of material, much of the detail is missing, so that it would not be possible to replicate exactly. For example, in the lesson described above we are not told exactly what happens when the teacher discusses the questions with the class, and – much more worryingly – it is unclear how the marks given are allocated. Pupil performance is given as follows:

Marks	Pupils
9–10	9
7–8	10
5–6	3
3–4	0
1–2	1
	23

(Madras girls, lesson 183, mimeo)

We are not told whether these marks represent two for each of the five true–false answers, or whether one mark is for the correctness of the answer and the other for the reason which students were asked to give, and, if so, how the latter was assessed. Such questions are important for the evaluation of the project, though the reporting so far has been avowedly interim, and it would be unfair to criticise the available notes for not being a formal basis for evaluation, as they are not intended for that purpose. It is possible, though, to predict certain problems in evaluation which will be difficult to avoid, if we are to evaluate the hypothesis in its strongest form.

· Most of the students taught have not been beginners (though there are reports of satisfactory progress by the one group of beginners, in Madras, starting 1981–2). The methods of teachers, especially when teachers other than Prabhu and his closest associates have been teaching, have tended to revert to structural procedures, and the materials – as the example cited shows – are often less revolutionary in design than the description of the programme might lead us to expect. Until recently, also, all the students taught have been girls.

Such criticisms can be answered, in part. If this is a project based on innovation in a specific situation, it is appropriate for it to be suggestive rather than conclusive in its relation to language-learning theory. Indeed, the implication of the research position on education outlined in Chapter 1 is that an attempt at any conclusive solution to hypotheses of an abstract kind would be inappropriate for genuine methodological research. Controlling teacher behaviour, it could thus be argued, would only destroy the organic relation between teaching behaviour of the past and any possible realistic development in the future, and would lead teachers to ignore the most central aspect of their work – the instinctive and constantly improvised and renegotiated relationship with their class as a social group. Hence, if teachers revert to the traditions with which they are most familiar, this does not invalidate the exercise as an attempt to innovate in a particular place with a particular curricular tradition. To decontextualise innovation, it could be argued, is to raise unanswerable questions about restoring connections with normal circumstances. At least, from this project, suggestions for adaptation to other circumstances can be derived, and similar projects can be set up – as, indeed, they have been in other parts of India. We could accept within our general thesis that only the lack of experiment with total beginners need be crucial for the basic position that Prabhu has adopted, in relation to his local conditions.

Other experimental problems remain: even the experienced Indian teachers are not typical Indian teachers; there is danger of Hawthorne effect; and it has been claimed that the flexibility in language demanded of teachers by this approach is unrealistic in the South Indian situation.

There has also been, in practice, some unwillingness to agree in advance about what would constitute falsification of the hypothesis. This probably results from uncertainty about the status of the project. It started out as an experiment, but it soon acquired a momentum of its own, as a result of the interest it created, and increasingly appeared to be a fairly large-scale piece of action research.[4] Nonetheless, it is necessary to place a time limit on the exercise, and in practice that has been imposed by the existence of an examination to be sat by all Standard VIII leavers. At this point, the experimental classes will be compared with the classes being taught by traditional methods, in a test designed to measure structural competence in English. Since Prabhu's hypothesis is that a problem-solving approach is effective in teaching the structure of the language, such a public examination should have some validity. It is also expected that more formal evaluation will be carried out, and some pilot studies were performed in 1981. But because it was either impossible or impracticable to control a number of major variables, as indicated above, it will be difficult to assess the precise significance of comparative results if they do not show major differences between the control and experimental groups.

It may be more sensible, then, to regard the Bangalore Project as an illustration of appropriate modification of language teaching in a spirit of enquiry, rather than as an experiment into the nature of language learning. At the same time, if results do turn out to be strongly in favour of the experimental group in particular language areas – or even if they are not strikingly against the experimental group – we shall need to look closely at the nature and sequencing of the materials to determine whether a developmental sequence of language structure is visible retrospectively. If there is no evidence of such a hidden sequencing, then there will be further major problems to explore concerned with how intellectual sequencing interacts with language development. While one possible cause of success, if the project is successful, could be the relative adequacy of the teachers used in the experimental classes set against possible inadequacies of teachers in control classes, further work should nevertheless pursue the original hypothesis in more controlled conditions. There is already evidence from alternative sources of the value of problem-solving activities specifically related to language, to the process of second-language acquisition (Winitz and Reeds, 1975), but any success with the Bangalore programme raises questions about problem solving as a process, rather than as a means of understanding the product, as it is used in the latter work.

Johnson (1982: 140–1) has pointed out that the conceptual development of Prabhu's 'procedural syllabus' suggests that it may be a covert semantico-grammatical syllabus. It is not in fact necessary for this to be so. The concepts with which Prabhu is concerned are not stated specifically, and while they may be sometimes realised in linguistic items (both lexical and semantico-grammatical), they will also appear as formal logical operations which may be realised as any of a large range of grammatical structures. Since the problems are embedded in knowledge of the world, as well as knowledge of the operations of the English language, the nature of the progression will not be defined by semantico-grammatical categories. Johnson's point may be just in relation to the implicit selection of some items in the procedural syllabus, but (unless a retrospective analysis reveals otherwise) it will not relate to the sequencing of the elements which is a necessary condition for the design, as distinct from the specification, of a syllabus.

On another point, though, Johnson is right to point out the dangers in Prabhu's scheme of heavy teaching at the pre-task stage. There is a considerable risk that this could turn into specific teaching of necessary linguistic items, discretely specifiable, but sequenced in accordance with the demands of the problems to be solved. If this happened – and it is still an open question whether this is inevitable in the hands of most teachers – the procedural syllabus would become simply a variant of 1(c) (ii) in our chart on page 95, but with selections from 1(a) interwoven with the educational syllabus. But the educationally directed syllabus which Prabhu uses is more abstract than that of most interdisciplinary programmes, for it is concerned with abstract problem solving and could reflect cognitive processes more starkly than any other form of content. If the programme is successful, and if a consistent pattern of cognitive procedures is reflected in the final ordering of materials, then we shall have the beginnings of a dimension of the analysis of *process*, which is not represented in the chart, and which will allow us to begin considering process developmentally in a way which is not provided by any of the product category systems that have so far dominated discussions of syllabus design.

6.4   Meaning and the language syllabus

We have seen, then, that the content of a language syllabus may be specified either in terms of the language itself, reflected in interactional or formal categories, or of syllabuses of meaning, reflected in socially appropriate content. We have seen, also, that it is the process of interaction itself which will determine, more than products of interaction, whether language is being experienced by learners, so that their creative construction capacities are most effectively exploited. While our present state of understanding of process rather than product is primitive, there remains the possibility of developing, by trial and error in the classroom, a more sophisticated appreciation of the interaction of the many elements that must contribute to the language development process. However, if we are to pursue an integrated model of language development, we cannot adopt a mode of sequencing which simply reflects the categories of observers, because the effect of this is to isolate language from its social goals and to treat it from the outside as no more than a curious biological phenomenon. The value of this for our understanding of language is considerable, but learners are not attempting to understand the phenomenon of language any more than swimmers are attempting to understand the phenomena of mass and weight. The proposals which demand the teaching of subject matter or of problem solving may appear to go part of the way to resolving this difficulty, but they are still treating the content as a means of learning a language in the abstract, unsituated. There is, however, another way of examining the content issue.

If we ask the question, 'What should it mean, in a particular society, to be an English-speaking member of that society?' we shall come close to defining a possible content for the teaching of English, which is intrinsic to the language being learnt, whether it is in a foreign- or second-language context. If the question cannot be answered, perhaps the irrelevance of the learning has been demonstrated, and the subject should disappear from the curriculum. But in practice, and especially with English, because of its unavoidable economic role in most parts of the world, some sort of answer may be devisable. In practice, also, it is true, much of the discussion of needs analysis has appeared to approach this question by specifying target behaviours, and incorporating such specifications in the syllabus. But target behaviours have also been interpreted in a phenomenon-analysing spirit, which has resulted in the isolation of functions and potential meanings from any integrated view of why language learning is desirable or necessary. If we are to demand that students in conventional school systems should put in sustained effort over a period of many years in the learning of a code which does not, in many cases, have an immediate function to perform, then the justification may need to be more than merely 'Should you ever need to, you will be able to perform certain predictable speech acts'. For the whole argument of the research examined in this study has been that, while we use speech acts in performing language, we do not perform language in order to use speech acts, or vocabulary, or syntax, or cultural information, or cognitive problem-solving processes, or even a combination of these. We use language to express ourselves, to relate ourselves to our environment, to get things done which we want to get done, to assist others to understand things that we want them to understand, and so on. But the relationship between 'I', the speaker, and 'it', the language, is creative, and the relationship between 'I' and 'you', my interlocutor, is negotiated through the first creative relationship.

Although the general educational changes quoted from Rubin at the beginning of this chapter are demands which are too vague to provide specific guidance, the responses of language teachers to such challenges have usually been purely at a technical level. Only Stevick (1976; 1980), of the writers whose work I cited in connection with these demands (in 6.1), has related his work to the need for a fully integrated response to linguistic extension, and he has not been concerned with the long-term teaching of languages in a formal educational system in either of his major discussions of the problem.[5] But if the conditions established by Naiman, Fröhlich, Stern, and Todesco and quoted on page 91 are to be realised in ordinary schools and nurtured in ordinary classrooms, then the first essential condition is that there should be material that learners should want to know about, information and ideas that they should want to obtain from teachers or one another, *in the target language*. This implies that such material should not be what is freely available in mother tongue, but that it should be devised in direct response to the situation of the home culture. That is to say that 'being an English user' in France is different from being an English user in Ghana, or Malaysia, or Quebec, or

110

Switzerland, and that the subject matter of English teaching in France should, in English syllabuses, directly reflect the historical and ideological relationships between France and English-speaking countries. Only by doing this can designers of language courses prevent there being a mismatch between the reasons for learning a language and the reasons for providing a language in the curriculum. A French learner of English is making a bid to join the community of French speakers of English. The nature and value of such a community in France provides the subject matter, both the formal content and social meanings, for English language learning in France. Language teaching remains, like any other kind of teaching, preparatory – but only a criterion for content development such as that outlined above will allow the possibility of direct relationship to moral, aesthetic, intellectual, ideological, or instrumental goals without alienating students from their own society.

This proposal may seem grandiose and unrealistic. But it is difficult to see what alternative criteria there are for the integration of foreign-language education with general educational goals, and without such an integration the possibility of exploiting the capacities of language learners to make structure out of making meaning will be enormously reduced. In the remaining parts of this study we shall examine this question more closely, using the framework of product and process analysis outlined here.

7 Language learning as an integrated process

7.1 Context for an integrated model

We are now in a position to outline a model for a methodology of second-
or foreign-language teaching which reflects current preoccupations in
theoretical and practical discussion. Before we attempt to do this, however, it will be helpful to summarise the argument so far, so that the status
and purpose of the model is clear.

We have argued that the process of understanding our acts as teachers
– that is, the process of understanding teaching methodology – is in principle the same process as understanding any other aspect of the world. But
because teachers operate as human beings interacting with other human
beings, there will be restrictions on the means available to test our hypotheses about the nature of language learning and teaching. We shall not be
able to control the many variables involved in the language-using process,
and it will not be possible for us to predict the ways in which language
may be used legitimately by learners, for language is not a system that is
possessed passively by learners and users, but one which they exploit to
the best of their abilities for purposes which are infinite and consequently
unpredictable. As methodologists, we bring to bear understanding deriving from relevant theoretical disciplines, from experimentation and
speculation, and also from our awareness of what it is to be a language
teacher, learner, and user. But at the same time, this understanding is not
formalisable, for there is a great deal we do not know about language use.
Some of the things that we do not know are in principle discoverable, but
many are dependent on the infinite variability in language use and
language behaviour which results from the interaction between knowledge of the language system and knowledge of the world. Because there is
no way in which we can predict the knowledge of the world that will be
held by any language users in the future (Popper, 1957: v–vi), we cannot
predict the uses of language that they will need, except in very general
terms. We cannot therefore base our teaching on precise identification of
the *product* of teaching, but we can concentrate on enabling learners to
use the language tokens presented in their language work for purposes
which they will develop themselves. This philosophical position is supported by acquisition studies in mother tongue, and by more speculative,

112

but nonetheless increasingly accepted hypotheses in second-language acquisition.

However tentative we wish to be about accepting the discussion of contemporary researchers – whether these are based on descriptive studies or on hypothetico-deductive arguments that are convincing but difficult to substantiate, such as Widdowson's distinction between reference and expression rules – we have a responsibility to experiment with methodological innovations which will reflect such discussion. Indeed, such experimentation will also provide valuable, though necessarily informal, feedback to research and speculation. However, the process of experimentation must be responsible, for we are operating in an area where change can have considerable effects on the educational, political, and economic prospects of the students in whose service methodology is devised. Consequently, while there may justifiably be a premium on divergent thinking in speculation and scientific investigation (Lakatos, 1970: 114; and, much more passionately, Feyerabend, 1975: 29–33), implementation in the world of schools and classrooms requires the more cautious approach of piecemeal engineering. But the characteristic of piecemeal engineering is not that it is never risk taking and hypothetical, but that it is not a wholesale overturning of everything from the past. In this respect, methodological innovation is like political innovation, and Popper's scepticism is appropriate.

But the only way to apply something like scientific method in politics is to proceed on the assumption that there can be no political move which has no drawbacks, no undesirable consequences. To look out for these mistakes, to find them, to bring them into the open, to analyse them, and to learn from them, this is what a scientific politician as well as a political scientist must do. Scientific method in politics means that the great art of convincing ourselves that we have not made any mistakes, of ignoring them, of hiding them, and of blaming others for them, is replaced by the greater art of accepting the responsibility for them, and of trying to learn from them and of applying this knowledge so that we may avoid them in the future.

(Popper, 1957: 88)

To achieve such an experimental but responsible attitude to methodology requires two major preconditions. One is administrative: an organisation of the teaching profession in any particular educational system that creates maximally sensitive channels of communication between all the arms of the profession – teachers, administrators, teacher trainers, curriculum developers, inspectors, examiners, and materials writers. The other is epistemological: the interpretation of research and discussion in terms which neither undermine the fundamental premises of the empirical and speculative work, nor result in categories which are regarded by most teachers as too esoteric or complex for serious examination. The more important the question addressed, the more likely it is that either of these results will have a dangerous impact on the education system, as can be seen in the well-documented discussion of the effect on teachers of Bernstein's work (Gordon, 1978) and Bernstein's own difficulties in extricating himself from his interpreters (Bernstein, 1969).

In spite of the difficulties of formalising an account of the nature of language acquisition, it is clear that an approach to language teaching which treats it as solely a matter of learning a linguistic system, in isolation from the uses to which the system may be put in assisting conceptualisation and facilitating person-to-person communication, will fly in the face of our knowledge of the behaviour of language learners in natural conditions, of our experience of much effective language teaching in formal conditions, and of the most widely accepted current theoretical models. At the same time, language-teaching classrooms, especially in foreign-language situations, are not designed to make it easy for teachers to operate with an emphasis on use rather than usage; and the traditional emphases of many educational systems will draw teachers towards a more or less meaningless manipulation of the linguistic code, heavily dependent on the textbooks which happen to be provided. Recognising, as we must, that most language teachers feel themselves – rightly or wrongly – to be overworked and underequipped with the facilities for successful communicative teaching, our task is to construct a model which will have the maximum possible effect in adjusting existing teaching towards processes compatible with a contemporary view of language learning. Clearly, any approach to such a task will rest on a fine judgement of how much or how little change it is realistic to expect of teachers in any given situation. But certain basic guidelines can be offered, which will be subject to finer adjustments in the light of local experience and needs. What are the basic principles that should underlie such guidelines?

The first principle is that guidelines should be explicit; the second, that they should be negotiable; and the third, that they should be limited in scope, which is to say that they should be weakly falsifiable.

i) *Explicit guidelines*: The basic principles, underlying assumptions, and objectives of any teaching programme should be made as explicit as possible, because if they are not made explicit they will prove impossible to object to, adjust, and improve. It is true that one of the possible dangers of explicit specification of objectives is a simplistic translation of the specification into teaching without reference either to learning theory or to the contribution of the student (see Dixon, 1967, for a discussion of this problem with reference to mother-tongue teaching). But this danger can be guarded against, and the alternative – a teaching programme which is never articulated – leaves us with no data on which to base any monitoring of the well-formedness or otherwise of the arguments underlying classroom selection and decision-making processes.

ii) *Negotiable guidelines*: Guidelines are provisional, subject to reappraisal, by any participant in the educational process, through public debate. They must inevitably represent a compromise between a number of different positions, for generalisations based on limited data will differ from generalisations based on more substantial data. The search for satisfactory guidelines is a search for the most appropriate level of generalisation for a particular educational setting. Thus guidelines may become fixed at the levels of international professional associations (in the form of a universally recognised 'approach': Anthony, 1963), or of Ministries of Education, or of particular schools, each one manifestly relating to guidelines operating at other levels, but each negotiated within the constraints of a particular type of professional need.

iii) *Limited guidelines*: If guidelines are not to acquire the status of once-and-for-all pronouncements, their limitations need to be spelt out. Wherever appropriate, we shall need to know how guidelines may be shown to be inadequate. Exactly what this will involve may vary. Some types of objective, for example, will be dependent on the demands of particular examinations, or institutions such as universities whose influence is historical rather than educational, and it should be clear that such objectives are related solely to the historical tradition, and would disappear if the relationship changed. Some innovations of materials or methodology will be dependent for their continuing use on success in realising teaching objectives. If this is so, an appropriate length of trial period needs to be stated. Only by such a specification of limitations will the distinction between essential elements in language teaching and conventional elements be maintained. Conventions may, and should, change, and we should be aware of the conditions that make change necessary wherever these can be made explicit.

7.2 The role of a product-based syllabus

It is logically impossible to conceive of an educational process without believing that learners are going to be changed in a desirable direction, and our criterion of explicitness demands that we should try to specify that direction as closely as we can. However, this is by no means a simple question, for – as we have seen – we should not expect to be able to specify exactly the language itself that students will expect to produce at the end of their course. At the same time, we have a general educational responsibility to be as clear-minded as we can (see White, 1982, for an argument for the specification of aims; also Stenhouse, 1975: 80–97; and Jeffcoate, 1979: 25–31, for a discussion based on second-language work). The most important question relates to the function of the specification. Stenhouse (1975: 81) relates the objectives model to 'Five verbs by Thursday!' but the relation need not be anything like as explicit as that. A list of language skills (such as that in Munby, 1978: 122–31) or a taxonomy of functions (such as that in Wilkins, 1976: 44–54) constitutes an explicit specification of linguistic product, and may be useful for four separate purposes. First, it may be valuable as a checklist for use in the testing of language, in order to ensure that reasonable coverage and distribution of language items has occurred in the devising of tests. Second, it may be valuable as a checklist for a syllabus, in order to ensure that a syllabus has incorporated all the elements felt to be appropriate for particular learners. Third, it may be valuable as a way of sensitising teachers to types of categories by which linguistic phenomena may be classified, and the criteria for the establishment of such a typology. And last, it may be valuable as a stated and public basis for the criticism of our view of language, and the effects of such a view on language teaching and learning. But there is no necessary relationship between the categories of analysis and the type of synthesis achieved by teachers in the classroom. It may be justified tactically to say that, because such specifications are misused and treated as the basis of teaching, without any clear synthesis taking place, we should avoid such listings. But the fault may lie in the ways in which teachers act on the specification, or – more theoretically – in the lack of a clear articulation of procedures for translation of abstract listings into concrete classroom behaviour; it cannot be held to lie in the act of attempting to make a specification. Indeed, without the specification it is difficult to see how the criticism of approaches to language teaching can proceed, for we shall have no criteria for measuring whether one kind of language performance is taking place at the end of our course rather than another, and thus of relating what is done to what is offered by the teaching programme. We may wish to teach the process, but we have to measure the product.

A syllabus, then, must be related to a direction of change. But it cannot be simply a specification of desired terminal objectives; if that is all that is provided, there will be no basis for influencing the process of learning. Education is predicated on the view that experience of an organised process enables learning to occur more effectively than disorganised experience does. If we make explicit the nature of that organisation – that is, construct a syllabus – we shall have a public object available for scrutiny and consequent improvement. But the means of reaching terminal objectives, compatible with the best available generalisations about language learning, need also to be made explicit, and these will entail consideration of the traditional syllabus activities of selection and sequencing (Mackey, 1965: 157), though whether there should be grading, and what it should be based on, will depend on the kind of learning theory espoused.

A syllabus will also have to operate in the real educational world, however, for its existence can be justified only as a document which leads to more effective teaching and learning. It is tempting to say that therefore it should be related to schools, teachers, and students as they actually are. This would not be entirely accurate, though, for education is about the process of change, and the whole argument of this study has been designed to support the view that the relationship between teachers and students – and indeed, between the whole educational system and students – is crucial to their development. Consequently, a syllabus provides also the framework for *teacher* change and development, and institutional development. There is thus a delicate balance between a specification which is so unrealistic as to prevent change, and one which is so conventional as to reinforce the past and equally to prevent change. The former is ignored because it is perceived to be irrelevant; the latter accords so well with current practice that it need scarcely be perceived at all. But curriculum designers usually have a personal interest in change, and the former danger is greater than the latter. Syllabus design and implementation, like politics, is the art of the possible, and it cannot demand changes, however desirable, which will not be taken up by practitioners.

We have, then, a product-based syllabus in order to ensure that there are some controls on the activity that takes place in the classroom. But it is clear that the syllabus must contain a process element, for otherwise it will not be a syllabus at all, but simply a statement of terminal behaviour of a restrictive kind. Furthermore, as we have seen from our examination of language acquisition and learning, any target specification will have only limited value: we cannot identify the target with what we are trying to teach. We are trying to teach an underlying capacity which will result in, among other things, the ability to perform as specified by target analyses. But we need to be able to think in a coherent way about what we are doing as teachers, and some students appear to need to think about what they are doing (Naiman, Fröhlich, Stern, and Todesco, 1978: 103). Even if we reject claims that the language system being learned should explicitly appear in the content of the syllabus, it will be difficult for teachers to think about what they themselves are doing over the period of several years that characterises most conventional school-based education unless they have some coherent structure to hold to. For them there appears to be a choice of either

i) an intrinsic system relating to what is to be learnt (1(a) or 1(b) in the chart on page 95); or

ii) an externally imposed structure in which the language is learnt peripherally, while a more motivating external pattern is apparent as the basis for overt learning (1(c) in the chart).[1]

Which of these two choices is made depends partly on learning theory, but also on face validity for teachers, and administrative possibilities. As we have seen, it is also possible to marry these two types of structure, and there are arguments in favour of both at the current stage of discussion (see Chapter 5).

What we have to be clear about is the limited role of any syllabus of this type, for – from the point of view of the language acquirer – it is the personal language activity which constitutes the acquisition process, and this activity cannot be prespecified in the syllabus. In terms of our accuracy/fluency distinction, the syllabus is always accuracy-based, for, while the syllabus is uppermost in the mind of teacher or learner, the emphasis will be on form or content as determined by an external specification of structure. It is only when the elements in the structure are being *used* for purposes accepted by the learner that they can be incorporated into the personal constructs of each learner, and simultaneously constrained by the conventional constructs that make communication possible. The syllabus, then, has to be seen as having two roles only. On the one hand, it is a means of activating and motivating the capacities of students to acquire language, and thus provides a structure for initial teaching of linguistic tokens (either as *language* items, or through *content* selection). On the other hand, it is a device to enable teachers to check coverage and appropriacy of material, so that adjustments can be made retrospectively and the long-term process of teaching can be monitored. In this sense it provides a basis for remedial work, correction, and revision in class, as well as self-awareness and renewal for teachers out of class. But the explicit role of the syllabus as an inventory of items will decrease as students develop their own systems, so that the relationship between accuracy and fluency will be as outlined in the diagram opposite.

The role in teaching of any syllabus for language learning should be limited to that within the shaded area.[2]

7.3 Integration of the model

Monitoring, resort to reference rules, accuracy work, and a concern for explicit knowledge are all essentially non-integrated activities, and consequently will not form the prime basis for normal language use. We have argued that, nonetheless, on pedagogical grounds, they have their place. At the same time, we would insist that all these reflect strategies resorted to by native speakers for some aspects of normal language use. But we cannot specify *how* learners are to integrate language elements; we can only provide opportunities for them to do so. What we have to say in relation to fluency work, then, will necessarily be at a high level of generality. But at the same time it is possible to specify the constraints within which fluency work should operate, with some precision, in terms of the analysis

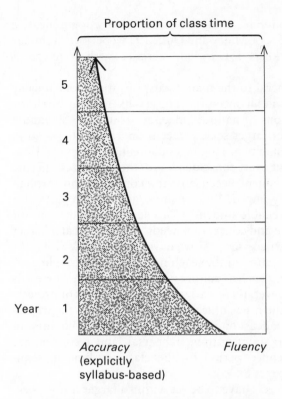

Fig. 2 *Schematic representation of class time spent on accuracy and fluency activities as a function of development from year to year*

of process in the chart on page 95, and to use a checklist for some additional categories.

We can, for example, make use of categories such as those in Munby (1978: 54–75) to ensure that opportunities may have been provided, through role play, for appropriate content, role relations, and situations – where these are highly predictable. But in practice such categories will operate most effectively as checklist items rather than as systematic input to the syllabus; that is, they provide convenient non-theoretically motivated lists[3] against which a consistently constructed syllabus can be checked, after initial drafting, to ensure that major convenient constellations of function, situation, and role have not been omitted. Similar checklists can be used to ensure that specific appropriate topics have been covered in developing skills in extended writing, or comprehension, if coverage is not sustained as part of a broader content programme, through interdisciplinary work, or the teaching of language, linguistics,

119

or culture. And more randomly, books of games, or of communicative exercises (such as Lee, 1965; or Maley and Duff, 1978), perform a similar function, acting as checklists for varied exercises with a range of purposes.

But all of this is peripheral to the main thrust of satisfactory fluency activity. For this, the traditional once-off exercise is likely to be too short-term, because the conditions of natural language acquisition demand a more extensive concern for larger-scale projects. Short activities tend to be focused on specific elements of language, content, or function. Even when they are used without overt consciousness of these features, specific elements will appear prominent because of the concentration through repetition or an artificially imposed information gap on one particular characteristic. In order to enable students to use language as determined by genuine communicative and conceptual needs, projects set at a higher level of abstraction will be necessary. As we have argued, these will most easily be set within the structure of the teaching of another discipline, or through substantive content such as culture or literature. Even where this is difficult to achieve, however, there are large-scale role plays or projects which can be adapted to the needs of learners. An example is the whole-class preparation for a broadcast on the characteristics of the country, in which planning, research, script-writing, rehearsal, and recording are carried out over an extended period by the class working in semi-independent groups (see pages 84–5).

But such integrated projects have to be set within a larger framework. Integrated, naturalistic fluency work will depend on two types of support for students. One will be access to the tokens of the target language, taught through presentation procedures of various, not necessarily traditional, kinds, and reinforced by the process of correction in the course of normal teaching. The other will be the provision of appropriate material as part of the projects themselves, whether they are part of a larger content syllabus or not. This material will operate as what Krashen has called 'optimal input', and will need to be comprehensible, interesting, relevant, and appropriately simple without being grammatically sequenced (Krashen, 1981b: 102–5). The learner will then operate as shown in the diagram on page 121.

In fact, of course, the appropriate material may be within a wide range of language, for students will be working in groups, and their own language ranges will vary considerably. Krashen's claim that 'the acquirer understands input that contains structures a bit beyond his or her current level of competence' (Krashen, 1981b: 102) is restrictive, both in failing to relate comprehension to extra-linguistic knowledge and in concentrating on the individual in isolation from the group. Matching a linguistic level in reading matter, however precisely graded, to the subtle, variable, and content-related interest on the part of a student, means correlating the

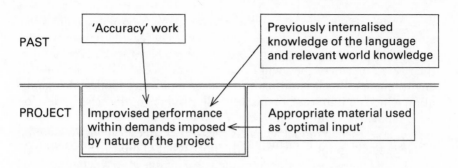

Fig. 3 Learner activity on a project

measurable with the immeasurable – an exercise that is logically imposs-ible. This does not constitute an argument against *communicative* simplification, but it does cast doubt on the determination to devote enormous effort to precise linguistic grading in isolation from all other factors.

But we can ensure that the structure of the language classroom enables students, through their engagement in small-group tasks, to understand materials of varying levels of sophistication, and to convert them to their own ends. The skilled teacher becomes adept at using the interactions between students as a means of grading material, especially when they are used to performing independently, with considerable freedom for manoeuvre. The language text thus becomes more than simply a piece of linguistic data, but a component part of a total linguistic interaction, in which the language may be literally incomprehensible in isolation from what is done with it and who does it; in other words, it becomes fully contextualised.

Fluency work thus becomes as similar as possible, in the foreign language, to much good practice in mother-tongue teaching, whether of the mother tongue itself or of other subjects.[4] Of course this will require appropriate materials as a resource, in the form of extensive reading materials, magazines, reference books, and so on. In many parts of the world these are fairly easily made available in school; in others, they could easily be made available if languages were treated as seriously as the sciences, or even if the money available for recording hardware was made available for cheap reading materials; in some parts of the world financial constraints may reduce this demand to something which is specifically textbook-based and much more limited in scope.[5] But what can be stated with confidence is that, unless students are able to have access to some such rich and continuing project-like activity, they will never have a language-using community in the class in which all students can participate. Other modes of class and material organisation will benefit some students, and – as past experience shows – will enable naturally competent language learners to develop to a point where they can continue on their own, or where they will eventually gain access to acquisition-rich environments. But it is difficult to conceive of other modes of organisation which contain the potential for all members of the class to develop their capacities as fully as they can.

We have, then, a model which asks as its first question not 'What kind of language is going to be needed?' but 'What should it mean to be a speaker of language X in this community?' This question will be answered only partly in terms of language. Crude issues of the relative importance of reading, conversation, and writing may be partially answered in responding to this question, but against these answers will be offset the pedagogical value of these activities. Far more, it will lead to discussion of the comparative value of such activities to students who may or may not travel to foreign countries, in relation to what they might usefully learn through the foreign language, or as a necessary corollary of trying to learn it. Such a question will be answered prescriptively, as any educational question should. The aims of language teaching should be negotiable, and capable of being argued with, but they should not be passively instrumental in a state educational system, for if there is no clearly justifiable reason for learning a foreign language, or a particular foreign language, reflected in the structure of the syllabus, students will perceive only too quickly that perhaps such teaching should not take place at all. There are plenty of alternative subjects which could be justified instead.

Only when this question has been answered will questions about the linguistic or process contents of the course become appropriate. Whether a design model should then be a cautious compromise between linguistic and communicative categories (Stern, 1981; Widdowson and Brumfit, 1981), more traditional, or more experimental, is a question for a separate argument, though, as we saw in Chapter 6, there is increasing interest in a compromise. What we do have to insist on is that the formal syllabus design must be subject to the more fundamental kind of questioning outlined above, and that the *processes* of classroom activity, which cannot by definition be prescribed in detail, must be given much greater prominence. Syllabuses themselves, while important, inevitably result in fragmentation insofar as they are specific, and they must be seen as servants of integrated goals and bases for integrated methodology. Only from goals which have some educational and content value will we achieve language courses that reflect current theories of the nature of language, because only when there are messages being carried which are significant to users will there be full engagement with the linguistic code. And only when opportunities for interaction and exploration are provided by the methodology will a sensitive, learner-centred procedure be possible.

The model for language-teaching methodology that we are proposing, then, is prepared to be unspecific, in a principled manner, wherever specificity would restrict teachers or students by predicting what should be spontaneous and prescribing what should be improvised. The most important conclusion from the research examined in this study is that the precise analysis characteristic of much linguistic research will be counter-productive if transferred unmediated to pedagogy. There are two reasons for this. The major one is that language is impossible to acquire if the product is predefined; what will then be acquired is merely language-like behaviour. A less theoretically significant, but nonetheless important, reason is that over-exact analysis will produce constructs which are at an inappropriate level of generalisation and sophistication to result in change in the educational system as a whole, for innovation which cannot cause motivated changes in the behaviour of teachers in their day-to-day activities will inevitably have only an indirect and distorted effect on the general practice of teaching and learning.

Our model for language-teaching methodology will look like this:

1 *Goal* To enable learners to use the target language they have acquired for any purposes they wish, and to be able to extend it as far as they wish.
(Constrained by the time limits of the course).

2 *Means* A specification of:
   i)   a substantive content in answer to the question: What should an (English)-speaking member of this community know in order to function most effectively? That is, what does it mean to be an (English)-speaking member of this community?

   ii) a linguistic content for initial presentation and systematic remedial work, to be developed by trial and error on the basis of past experience of teaching similar groups.

3 *Methods*
   i)   A fundamental recognition of the distinction between accuracy and fluency work, and the allocation of a role for fluency work similar to that in the diagram on page 119.

   ii) Variation between the processes classified on page 96 both in reinforcement accuracy work, and in fluency activities, constrained only by the specification made under 2 (ii) above;

   iii) Increasing emphasis on integrated projects in which the content will be specified by 2 (i) above and the classroom organisation arising more and more from the communicative needs of students within the framework of the projects – constrained, however, by the general availability of materials and the administrative framework of schools.

[Model of language-teaching methodology]

Comments

1 *Goal*: The goal does not specify the form of language used at all. Because of the difficulties in communicative testing (Morrow, 1977; Carroll, 1980), there may be specifications either of linguistic or functional content for the purposes of publicly accountable evaluation, but this is simply the traditional conflict between student-centred and society-centred goals implicit in any education – we can only ever measure an ability or capacity by testing specified products of that ability. Nonetheless, we are aiming to produce a capacity to perform, not a specified type of performance.

2 *Means*: (i) The substantive content will lead to decisions under 1(c) of our chart on page 95 concerned with whether teaching should aim at courses on British, American, Australian, or other culture (see Strevens, 1977a: 133),[6] whether it should be interdisciplinary or immersion, or directed more academically at language or literature. Such factors will of course be measured against the types of student, and courses will also be possible based on combinations of these elements. Our argument differs from previous discussions of language teaching, however, in insisting that these decisions are central to the development of language teaching, and should not come in merely as an optional afterthought.

(ii) We have argued that a specification of linguistic content is still desirable, but we include 'communicative' specifications related to role, situation, functions, and notions as 'linguistic'. Such specifications may appear traditional, or may accord with the most recent discussions of syllabus definition and design. Our major argument is that the form of syllabus specification is less important than the type of activity – and above all, the type of relationship encouraged between the user and the process of use. Syllabuses specify linguistic tokens; learning a language is learning to negotiate the *value* of these tokens in a culture to which the speaker contributes.

3 *Methods*: (iii) The demand for integrated projects is the only demand which requires a commitment, for any type of school system, for resources greater than those already provided. Yet it would be foolish and unrealistic not to indicate the potential of such an approach. Furthermore, many features of project work can be developed with limited resources, and many projects can be developed out of materials which are either non-linguistic or available freely through local commercial or diplomatic agencies.

This study has argued the justification for approaching language teaching in this way. The exact details of implementation of each of the goals, means, and methods outlined above will be dependent on discussion between participants in the educational process, for any institution or educational system. But there are compelling arguments for approaching the teaching of languages in this way, operating within a broad framework of this kind. In the final chapter we shall look at some possible objections, and at some of the specific implications of this approach for contemporary discussion of language teaching.

8 A fluency-based model of language learning: problems and implications

8.1 Research and administration

In this final chapter we shall accept the argument made so far, and explore as carefully as we can the implications for current language teaching, though in terms of general principles, not of specific practices; we are not making universal claims for details of practice. This will inevitably lead us to explore many problems implicit in the argument, and will force us to follow the precepts set out in Chapter 1 and to consider the major possible criticisms of this model as a realistic and practical basis for second- and foreign-language teaching.

In Chapter 1 we developed an argument, which was summarised in Chapter 7, about the role of research in the development of policy for methodology of teaching. The demand for a fluency-based language-teaching methodology does not depend on this argument, but it is important to note that the source of ideas in language teaching is significant both for our discussion of the nature of 'knowledge' about how to teach effectively, and for the particular solutions proposed. This study derives to a considerable extent from teaching experience recollected in, if not tranquillity, at least the relative freedom from the immediate demands of the next lesson. In part, it has developed out of a desire to make sense of a teaching experience, by the examination of relevant research, the exploration of procedures informally in various different teaching situations, and analysis of the experiences of other teachers whose ideas shed light on the nature of language and of language teaching. We have not been approaching language teaching as if it were a manifestation of organised linguistic behaviour – as data for a consideration of a theory of language. Nor have we been trying to control the variables and produce evidence which would be difficult, or even impossible, to relate to the confused situation of typical language teaching in typical schools. What we have tried to do is to maintain the stance of the teacher, but to use research and theoretical discussion from whatever source appears to be relevant, in order to develop a coherent view which both reflects contemporary research and theory without gross distortion, and corresponds to a view of the classroom as seen by a practitioner of *teaching*, rather than, say, quantitative research, or hypothetico-deductive discussion. This is not, of course because no role is seen for either of these other activities – indeed, we have made use of the work of scholars in these traditions in the course of this study – but because the attempt to do the kind of work described here has been neglected academically, while we expect teachers all the time to be performing such a task of integration and synthesis in their professional activity. Consequently, even bad examples of how we might integrate insights from the various disciplines which can contribute to our understanding of language teaching will be valuable in providing models to be responded to and rejected and ideas for improvement or refinement. Furthermore, we have argued, successful innovation in teaching depends on a close integration between advisory services, research, and the practice of teaching. The process of mediation is itself creative, and represents one aspect of that renewal of connection without which the work of linguists will degenerate into aestheticism.

One result of the dissatisfaction with experimental studies of teaching methodology, referred to in 1.3, has been greater scepticism about the role of 'science' in the formulation of principles for effective teaching. Indeed, language teaching has moved along with general educational discussion towards a greater concern for a holistic view of the human personality, 'humanistic' values, and a less analytical approach to the subject matter of teaching. To a considerable extent, this study fits in with such a movement. But there are dangers in an approach which can easily degenerate into untidy or sloppy thinking, especially when we are working in a field which is incapable of formalisation. But at the same time, there are greater dangers in pursuing a false formality. Ultimately, a view of human activity which claims to be able to formalise the *particular* is based on the false historicism criticised in Popper (1945), while we have tried to argue in this study that a view of human activity which only makes *general* statements will pose insuperable problems to teachers who have to translate general statements into particular actions for particular learners.

The most appropriate procedure for advancement of our understanding of language-teaching methodology is to combine statements about the nature of language teaching which are explicit and open in their argument with administrative machinery for the activation of the profession in any educational system. Open and easy channels for communication, regularly used, in which all teachers have access to a common language and system of concepts, both of which are negotiable enough to be able to accommodate new ideas but at the same time stable enough to allow the possibility of maximum communication and discussion, are a major safeguard against the dangers of sloppy thinking. The organisational issue cannot be separated completely from the scientific issue, so long as we are concerned with producing teaching that is effective in the world as it is.

It may be claimed that this view is too optimistic. Many Marxists, for example, would argue that the effect of such organisational safeguards is to reinforce the status quo and to neutralise radical change. But I would wish to insist on a concern for the world as it is. Again, the argument is Popperian, and was outlined in Chapter 7. The risks of a desire for wholesale change are too great. We have to assume that teachers in general are committed, sensitive, and intelligent people, both because only if we do act on this assumption can we expect them to be so, and because if they are not, the whole exercise will fail because we could not expect such people to implement the committed, sensitive, and intelligent procedures devised by outsiders. There are limits to the impact that teacher trainers, methodologists, and applied linguists can expect to have on the teaching profession – the relationship between discussion such as this study, and the process of teaching, like the relationship between theory and practice, must be symbiotic. We may wish to subscribe to a cautious radicalism, but the caution is as important as the radicalism, at least in formal state educational settings, if we do not want to exploit either students or teachers. The Popperian model provides a suitable basis, on these grounds.

A more probable objection to this insistence on organisational matters is that of expense. A really serious commitment to strong professional teachers' organisations, strong, subject-based advisory and support services, and fully utilised professional journals, is a commitment in both time and money. This argument is difficult to counter, except by insisting that such a commitment is no more expensive than many, intellectually more impressive-sounding, research projects which are too 'pure' to have any true impact on teaching, and that there is no substitute for such a commitment. However much we might like to, we are never going to 'prove' that particular educational procedures are, in all circumstances, preferable to all other possibilities. We do not have to choose between a false and unattainable reliance on science and experiment on the one hand, and the inertia of conservatism resulting in a stagnant educational system on the other. We can choose the fullest support for an active teaching profession which has facilities for the exchange of information, informal experimentation, and action research,[1] and genuine argument between practitioners and observers. In fact, though this is not an appropriate place to spell such proposals out in detail, such channels of communication and professional organisation need not be particularly difficult or expensive to organise. But it is important for our argument to see that there are unavoidable administrative consequences of our position.

The position that we have argued here on sources of understanding of language teaching is beginning to be acknowledged by researchers who start from non-teaching perspectives. Krashen, whose position, as we have seen, has important parallels with that taken up here, has argued in his most recent book (Krashen, 1982: 2–4) that our attempts to improve language teaching rely on information from second-language acquisition research, applied linguistic research (by which he appears to mean comparative studies of different methods) and the experience of the teaching profession. While we may feel that he undervalues the role of research in areas other than psycholinguistics, and perhaps overvalues the possibilities of making generalised statements about particular teaching methods, nonetheless it is clear that this position resembles the one we have taken in this study. However, for such a position to be held consistently, it is necessary for the information derived from these various sources to be synthesised, and that in itself is, as we have seen, a difficult and time-consuming operation which raises many problems. We may wish to claim, indeed, that the process of communication between teachers and researchers demanded earlier in this argument is dependent on large numbers of studies being produced, of this kind, in which teaching experience is allied to examination of the relevant literature, rather than on teachers being expected to work within an experimental or data-based paradigm when they are engaged in research. A true intercommunication must consist both of those trained as researchers working as teachers and those trained as teachers engaging in research, and also of those who have had extensive experience of teaching exploring the significance of research and theoretical discussion.

8.2   Fluency distinguished from accuracy

Our discussion in Chapter 2 of the nature of language and of language acquisition and learning has led to two important and widely accepted conclusions. The first is that descriptive categories, such as most of those used by linguists, miss out an important dimension of language when it is examined from the perspective of the learner: we do not receive language passively – we create it and construct it, constrained on the one hand by our need to make sense of the world for ourselves, and on the other hand by the need to operate conventions which will enable us to communicate effectively with those around us. The reification of categories resulting from language being conceived of, by linguists, as an object 'out there', inevitably diminishes the creative and ideological role of the language user. The second conclusion is that language cannot be isolated from the many other factors which help to create human personality and the societies within which these operate. The possible uses of language are infinite and unpredictable. We are not learning to use a specific tool, like a saw, but the principles of tool construction, ready for any purpose we may eventually decide upon – but tool construction constrained by the need to interact with other people who are engaged in the same task.

We have discussed many of the implications of the accuracy/fluency distinction in Chapters 3, 4 and 5. It is my contention that by exploring this topic during teacher-training courses, and by using it as the basic conceptual distinction in the discussion of teaching methodology, a methodology consistent with the most coherent contemporary theory will be developed more effectively than by the use of other categories. One reason for making this claim is that the distinction operates at a high level of generality, and is therefore capable of generating a hierarchy of subsidiary procedures under each heading, which will be adaptable to local conditions, and will also – via these two categories – be related to fundamental types of linguistic behaviour in the classroom. Thus the kinds of grammar exercises criticised by Widdowson (1978a: 112–15) will fit clearly within the accuracy category, because it would not be possible to work with them except from a desire to manipulate the linguistic code consciously. An exercise like 'Blurred focus' (Maley, 1981: 139)[2] would clearly be fluency work because the activity could not be performed with a prior specification of the linguistic code by either teacher or student. Other types of exercise, such as that in Widdowson (1978a: 127) in which students complete a diagram by classifying gases, liquids, metals, and (rather curiously) instruments, and placing the names in appropriate boxes will provoke interesting discussion, for the mental set of students may be the determining factor – in that if this is seen as a classification exercise, it might be regarded as fluency work, but if it is simply a vocabulary test for those who have no problem of classification, it is certainly accuracy. Such discussion will raise important issues of the role of overt language activity in a language which is already known, and the relationship between language and concept. The point about the distinction is that it is theoretically motivated, but at the same time corresponds to a basic, intuitive understanding possessed by most learners and teachers.

Because the distinction is relatively simple to grasp in its essentials, generalisable, and theoretically derived, it is likely to provide a better basis for the systematic thinking about the planning of teaching than more random suggestions. Morrow (1981: 60–5), for example, in a brief discussion of communicative methodology, adduces five principles:

1 Know what you are doing;
2 The whole is more than the sum of the parts;
3 The processes are as important as the forms;
4 To learn it, do it;
5 Mistakes are not always a mistake [*sic*].

While there is no question that the discussion in this paper is pertinent and accessible, it is worth pointing out that (1) and (4) do not particularly relate to communicative rather than any other language-teaching approach, and that only (5) and possibly (3) specifically relate to the kind of theoretical discussion about the nature of language that we have been engaged in here.

The advantage of working with the accuracy/fluency distinction is that, unlike with the kind of principles suggested by Morrow, it is possible to ask a teacher for the objective of any classroom activity in terms of the distinction, and to argue about the appropriateness of the activity in relation to a view of the nature of language learning and of the requirements of pedagogy. Furthermore, the distinction is neutral with respect to the type of syllabus specified, but insists that the syllabus can influence only one part of the language work. Accuracy will tend to be closely related to the syllabus, will tend to be teacher-dominated, and will tend to be form-based. Fluency must be student-dominated, meaning-based, and relatively unpredictable towards the syllabus. By giving the latter prominence, without completely rejecting the former, motivation is provided for the selection of process activities (Morrow, no. 3), for deciding what are 'mistakes' and when a mistake is a mistake (no. 5), for concentrating on the whole rather than the parts (no. 2) and for the nature of doing (nos. 1 and 4). Only by promoting such an emphasis can we expect teacher decision making in methodology to acquire the same prestige as administrator decision making in syllabus design, or examiner decision making in test construction.

But it may be argued that an emphasis on fluent language activity of this kind may result in the development of fluent pidgin, but not of a fully fledged language system, capable of being used with maximum, native-language-like efficiency. There may be some defence to be made for a view that a fluent pidgin is preferable to non-fluency, but it is probably fair to concede that, for conversation at least, this must remain an important empirical question for our argument. Only experience of using this approach will resolve this question fully: if teachers feel that a heavy emphasis on fluency is resulting in deficient conversational abilities compared with reliance on other procedures, they will no doubt adjust to the other procedures for the good of their classes. From our position, it is only important that such failures should be fully reported, but we do need to be sure that if such results do occur, they are actually deficient compared with the alternatives. There is at the moment, in many places, little evidence of conversational capacities being successfully developed except where some sort of fluency-type activity is already available – as, for example, in second-language settings. Anyway, we need to be sure that the argument is clear, and this particular argument is surrounded by conceptual confusion.

Corder, in papers collected in Corder, 1981, has examined the relationship between language teaching, pidgins, and other reduced languages more closely than any other scholar. The significant difficulties with the concept of pidginisation are brought out in a paper where he insists that

'Pidginization is a linguistic, *not* a psycholinguistic process, and cannot properly be used to refer to the process whereby pidgins are created by speakers of other languages acquiring them on the basis of exposure to the data of the superstrate language' (Corder, 1981: 110). The well-documented possession by language learners of grammars which can be described as simple by linguists cannot be held to show that learners are actually engaged in a process of simplifying the target language, Corder maintains, for of course they do not have the knowledge of the target language to enable them to start simplifying it.

But learners do have the capacity to isolate salient features of the target language in relation to their most urgent communication needs (Hatch, 1978); and the relationship between selection, stereotyping, simplification, and systematising data to which we have been exposed is complex and little understood. What is clear, as Corder's work has shown over a long period, is that as language users we possess capacities to simplify and complicate within the systems that we have acquired. And since these systems are permanently changing by expansion (and indeed contraction, though this has been far less studied – see Bromley, 1966: 321), there is likely to be a relationship between such processes and the extension of our linguistic capacities.

What remains unclear is whether the process of fossilising is possible for a complete linguistic system, given that the user of the system is constantly presented with the conditions of use and motivation to exploit these conditions. Certainly, if simplified systems can be effectively used for major communicative purposes, we do not need to object to their appearance in the classroom,[3] unless they can be shown to prevent the necessary development of more complex systems. There is no evidence at the moment to support the view that this may happen, other than anecdote, though the debate on language deficit is related to this issue (Labov, 1969; Bernstein, 1971; Stubbs, 1980: 139–60).

We have seen, then, that pidgins share some features with interlanguages, but are functionally distinct. Corder has argued that they must be psychologically distinct, and indeed that the concept of pidginisation is inappropriately applied in psycholinguistics. In order to give force to the argument about the risks of fluent classroom pidgin developing, we should have to accept the notion of a whole linguistic system remaining stable even when varying communicative demands were made on it. As yet, we have no grounds to consider this likely, especially when the course monitors itself with an extending, formally-based syllabus in the accuracy component, and when learners will be exposed to written text (plus, through the language of teachers and recorded materials, spoken text in most places), extending the linguistic model far beyond the confines of what can be developed by the learners working as a private classroom language community. At the same time, we have to recognise that this is a possible risk, and monitor performance with this possibility in mind.

One other point deserves emphasis before we leave the issue of dangerous simplification, and it arises directly out of the last point. A classroom which is built around input from extended text, whether spoken or written, will result in comprehension and interpretation which will frequently be generalised and simplified. We do not usually think in terms of pidginisation of comprehension, and the concept may well be inappropriate for the reason that Corder has given. But any consideration of simplification must recognise the interrelationships between comprehension and production, and demand some sophistication of comprehension – if necessary, perhaps through accuracy-based intensive reading exercises, before concluding that production has stabilised at an inappropriately simple level.[4]

The other major difficulty advanced by opponents of free discussion is that students in monolingual classes will always use the mother tongue, especially when the language demands stretch them – that is, exactly at those moments when we hope they will experiment and stretch their target-language capacities. This is undoubtedly a practical problem to be overcome, but there are only two points worth making here. The first is that there is nothing intrinsically stranger about talking in a foreign language in a foreign-language class than there is about reading or learning vocabulary or any other of the traditional activities of such classes. If such a procedure assists learning, it will be justified in the eyes of both teachers and students, except for those who are uninterested in learning – and they will have the same problem with any other of the possible activities. The second point is that many teachers do effectively enable their students to use the target language for such purposes. There is no doubt that the teachers must engage their full powers in relating to the students, exploiting a wide range of techniques in order to demonstrate the value of the approach, and grading the tasks so that students do not have too much demanded of them too early – but this is no more than to say that experienced and skilled teachers are better than inexperienced and unskilled ones. If the procedure we have outlined is worthwhile, there is no doubt that, given commitment, it can be exercised by any competent teacher.

8.3 Fluency and serious content

In Chapters 6 and 7 I have argued that, for fluency to become as important a concept in language-teaching methodology as it needs to be, a concern for content will also be important. This is partly because content provides a systematic basis upon which the development of meaning can be built, and partly because content is likely to motivate learners more effectively than the system in isolation. At the same time, though, we have to recognise that many teachers have had severe reservations about too heavy an emphasis on content in language teaching, and this proposal may well be seen to be retrogressive.

It is certainly true that in both foreign-language teaching (Kelly, 1969; Howatt, 1984) and mother-tongue teaching (Shayer, 1972) language work has often tended to converge with the teaching of a body of content, such as literature or elementary linguistics. Furthermore, there may well be conflict between the worth of the subject matter and the overt intention in teaching a foreign language if it is claimed that we are merely using the content in order to do something else – teach the language. For this reason there are only two ideal alternatives: either to use immersion, and claim that the language is being learnt incidentally while another equally worthwhile subject is taught; or to find subject matter which can arguably reinforce the understanding of the language. This is the attraction of literature and culture courses.

But the dangers of too firm a content orientation still remain. It is often easier to test memorisation of content than operation of a linguistic system – or, indeed, operation of skills associated with the development of abilities in subject areas such as history or literature. In fact, the discussion of content subjects at all raises difficult problems, as we saw in our discussion of Hirst's work on modes of knowledge in 1.2. Insofar as the ability to operate in a discipline means the ability to use concepts in a particular way, the content will always be less important than the mode of thinking associated with it, and that mode of thinking will be frequently expressed most economically through language. The use of content in the developing of second or foreign languages may be associated with an increased emphasis on the role of language in education as a whole in its central position as a mediator and creator of new ideas (Britton, 1970; Hirst, 1974: 83; Barnes, 1976). Certainly, a major place for fluency activity will imply that foreign-language teaching sees itself as having educational objectives which are closer to those of other subjects than they have often been seen to be in the past. However, this area is fruitful for speculation, and not – at the present stage of discussion – available for systematic examination, and is best left as an indication of possible future development.

Within our present model, it is necessary to recognise the force of possible dependency on content factors, and to insist that the role of knowledge is to facilitate competence in the language, not to be a substitute for it. At the same time, though, close attention to the kinds of knowledge relevant to learners of a particular foreign language does give us a principled way of considering language syllabuses, rather than simply techniques or bodies of material which can only be analysed lesson by lesson. The natural unit for the construction of learning languages must be a large-scale unit such as a syllabus for a term, a year, or even longer, and not the single events of the lesson, or the brief sequence of the short course. This is because there is no evidence for a view that we learn language as a whole in the short stab of a single event. All the features that we have described making this a complex and long-term process force us to demand that the organisation of language teaching should assume long-term contact between student and target language. While a 'free' methodology may be applied to any kind of syllabus, the content syllabus does enable us to discuss the organisation of meaning in such a way that students will be aware of progression from one year to the next. For example, in a literature course, decisions about the ordering of books in the syllabus will not be taken solely on grounds of the language of the books, but will also take into account a range of other factors. These may include:

i)   cultural familiarity of the ways of life presented;
ii) intellectual level of arguments presented;
iii) complexity or transparency of the literary mode itself;
iv) accessibility of literary devices exploited by the author.[5]

These factors will be added to other types of pedagogical grading, such as the basic, but nonetheless very important issue of the length of the text. Such factors provide a basis for a development of understanding of the nature of literature, in principle isolable from purely linguistic issues, which will enable the sophistication of semantic development to be approximately graded. Since we are concerned with enabling students to operate a linguistic system which they are themselves creating in order to understand and communicate with increasing sophistication, a grading of content in terms of sophistication and complexity is desirable. But such a grading need not be precise; indeed, it can be precise only when we are dealing with relatively simple, linear operations which are unlikely to stretch students' linguistic capacities appropriately.

We should note, of course, that the example given here of literature will be appropriate only for certain classes. In principle, there is no limit to the range of possible subject matter once we have defined our groups of students. But all subject matter within an academic education will raise issues of grading of the same type as those noted for literature, while within other types of education the choice of subject matter – defined by our question of what should be known by a user of English in the particular setting – will determine the appropriate conceptual expression in English. Only through a consideration of content can we prevent a catalogue of semantic elements (whether notions, vocabulary items, or any other classification) from being presented independently of its relations to the system of the language in use.

It may appear that this argument conflicts with much recent discussion about specific language-teaching courses (Strevens, 1977b; Holden, 1977; Mackay and Mountford, 1978; Robinson, 1980). It does indeed conflict with the view that we either can, or should, teach students language for purposes that can be absolutely predicted. But it should be clear from the whole of our preceding argument that (except in the limited sense that language-like behaviour can be induced for highly stereotyped interactions) the language system of the learner will always transcend the limitations of the contexts in which it has been taught insofar as it is developing as a genuinely generative system. Our prime concern has been to define ways of exploiting students' capacities in this direction through the methodology that teachers use. Consequently, there is no real conflict. The short-term introductory courses (Cross, 1980) or the highly specific courses such as those outlined by Munby (1978: 190–204) may have a place in the school system, but only as introductory or rescue courses in which the aim is to teach a limited code of quasi-language, either to motivate learners to go further, or to solve a particular urgent, and probably temporary, need. The more academic study-based courses may still be justified, but by reference to our content criterion. The breaking down of language courses into specific units, however, with mastery of each stage being desired before the next one is attempted, may be incorporated into our model as a way of structuring much of the accuracy work, but will conflict if extensive fluency activity is not also allowed.

The goal of the teaching process explored in this study, for most students, will be an ability to do anything they need to in the target language – reading, conversing, listening, or writing – but in a form which will progress from being markedly non-native learner towards an acceptable international standard. 'An acceptable international standard' will involve being more or less indistinguishable from native speakers in relevant writing tasks, ability to comprehend native and non-native speakers, and ability to communicate, while still, like native speakers, remaining clearly marked for place of origin in speech. But, from the arguments advanced here, it is difficult to sustain the view that learners can acquire and operate a limited language for a wide range of ever-extending purposes. As the purposes and range extend, so too should the capacity of the learner in the foreign language. The fundamental problem is how to develop procedures and planning which will motivate learners to extend their purposes and range.

And the answer to this problem, we have suggested, is to treat language teaching, as well as language learning, as a continuous process of self-adjustment, through a constant reappraisal of its relations with all available research and discussion. This is what this book has attempted to do.

Notes

Chapter 1

1   It should be noted that the interpretation of this aspect of Vico's work is notoriously difficult. Pompa (1981: 26–7) lists four interpretations: an inductive derivation of sociological principles, Croce's view of Vico's principles as a set of a priori categories, a set of truths about ourselves available through introspection, and Berlin's empathetic position cited here. For the argument of this study, it is not necessary to depend on ancient authority, so the debate is only peripherally relevant. But the concern, which may be attributed to Vico, and certainly can be attributed to Berlin, is a useful addition to our attitude to understanding teaching.

2   More recently Feyerabend (1975: 165–6) argues that the two processes must interact with each other; indeed, the process of proving *is* sometimes the process of making a new discovery. But even he agrees that there may be sharp differentiation, and an institutionalised confusion of the two would lead to chaos for much science and education.

3   Feyerabend's 'anarchy' (1975: 29–33) would seem to fit in with Popper's position here – a point developed in Chapter 7. Indeed, Stove (1982) unites Popper, Feyerabend, Kuhn, and Lakatos as anti-rationalists because they refuse to say that theories are 'right' or 'wrong'.

4   Compare also the similar extrapolation performed by Skinner (1957; 1971), and the complaints against orthodox psychology in L. Hudson (1972).

5   See the arguments developed by Popper to show that any prediction of human *behaviour* in the future must be misconceived, for we have no way of predicting future knowledge (if we could, it would no longer be future knowledge), and human behaviour must in part depend on the knowledge available to human actors. Ochsner (1979) for similar reasons distinguishes two scientific traditions – nomothetic and hermeneutic – and argues that both should contribute to second-language acquisition research. See also Hoetker (1975) with reference to teaching methodology.

6   See Dixon (1967) for discussion of a 'process model' in mother-tongue teaching; Breen and Candlin (1980) for a refusal to specify content in foreign-language teaching.

7   In later papers Freedman (1976; 1982) has tried to show that small-scale experimentation can resolve the difficulties of large-scale work. But the more carefully controlled the experiment, the greater the problems of translation to normal circumstances, and this does not seem to be a useful solution.

Chapter 2

1   It is worth pointing out that there is a problem with Halliday's position, at least until he is able to demonstrate a fully systematic form–function relationship, for there is no necessity for the form to relate precisely to functions for a linguistic system to operate effectively, and there is a danger of reductionism in his model. The competence/performance distinction allows for the examination of the code independently of its operation by users, and ultimately depends on a recognition of the arbitrary relation between, not simply words, but also all linguistic structures and their meanings. By refusing to allow the distinction, Halliday commits himself to a grammar motivated specifically by the uses to which it is put. Unless he allows *some* isolable and independent relationships (which could be idealised into a competence-based system), he risks sucking every feature of language into a communicative, meaning-committed network which would fail to allow for the possibility of innovation and creativity.

2   'Communicative competence' is defined in different terms by each of the authors referred to (see Munby, 1978: 21, for a schematic representation of various positions on this issue). For our purposes, though, it will be adequate to note that they are all objecting to the view that competence in the language can be usefully restricted to the ability to recognise or produce grammatical sentences in the language. Olson (1977) indeed argues that Chomsky's theory of language 'can serve as a theory of speech only when the sentence meaning is a fully adequate representation of the speaker's meaning. In ordinary conversational language, this is rarely the case' (p. 271). He claims, therefore, that Chomsky has produced a theory of writing – though this ignores several of the other difficulties we have outlined.

3   Compare, for example, the use of 'hockey' versus 'field hockey' in Canadian English, and 'ice hockey' versus 'hockey' in British English. See also Humboldt's view of language: 'No one when he uses a word has in mind exactly the same thing as another' (*Gesammelte Schriften* 4: 396, quoted in Sweet, 1980: 409); and 'Language is not a finished product: *Ergon* but creative activity: *Energeia*' (*Gesammelte Schriften* 7: 45–6, quoted in Sweet, 1980: 468). Also the German philosopher, G. Gerber, in *Die Sprache und das Erkennen* (Berlin, 1884: 161, quoted in Schmidt, 1976: 661): 'Words do not have just one meaning, but rather represent areas of meaning, whose periphery is constantly being determined, but never reaches an exact determination as long as the language of the word lives.' Only in the 'active desire to comprehend' does the text acquire meaning. This point can also be related to Popper's argument about the impossibility of predicting future knowledge (Chapter 1, note 5 above), for a view of language such as we have just outlined suggests that future meanings are always indeterminable.

4   This point is frequently made in the research on learning to read, for example, Goodman (1969) and F. Smith (1975: 92–5).

5   Widdowson (1981) expands at some length on the process of negotiation in attempting to buy two cheese sandwiches. Another example would be asking the way:

– Excuse me, could you tell me the way to the National Gallery?

– Yes, do you know how to get to Charing Cross Road?

– No.

– Well, it's the second on the right. Go down there until you come to Trafalgar Square. You know what Nelson's Column looks like?

etc.   (See also Schegloff, 1972, for further examples.)

An interesting historical example of self-consciously un-negotiable language is reported by Burke (1981: 25), when he reports that a Roman beggar arrested in 1595 told the authorities that there would be a general meeting of beggars the following May to change their slang because outsiders could now understand it.

6   For a sympathetic account of the 'critical-period' issue, see Slobin (1979: 124–6). For criticisms, see Christopherson (1972: 44–51); Krashen (1981a: 70–82).

7   The terms 'accuracy' and 'fluency' have been used to express a similar polarity by Wigdorsky (1972), Howatt (1974), and Sutherland (1979), but none of them has developed the implications of the distinction in the way outlined here.

Chapter 3

1   Implicit in Quintilian (1920), Book I, 1, 10 and 12, where it is stressed that children will learn the language of their slave nurses and grow up with Greek first, coming to school knowing both Greek and Latin. See also Lewis (1977: 61–3).

2   We should perhaps note that this distinction will correspond closely to the distinction between writing and speech.

3   Though in Krashen (1982) he is again quite categorical: 'A very important point that also needs to be stated is that learning does not "turn into" acquisition' (p. 83).

4   I have preferred to retain the terms 'reference' and 'expression' as in the 1978 version of this paper, rather than 'code' and 'context', to which they have been altered in book publication (Widdowson, 1979: 184). The original terms, I suggest, express more clearly the *process* which is held to cause the difference in product.

5   The relationship with teachers' traditional behaviour enables us to allow that this distinction may reflect experiential knowledge of the kind discussed in 1.1.

6   Note the fusion, appositionally, of 'formal' knowledge and 'conscious' learning in this quotation. There is, of course, no necessary relationship between formalisation and conscious learning, but it is necessary for Krashen's separation of what is learnt from what is acquired for this to be so.

7   This represents, together with the refusal to correct found in methodologies derived from this position (for example, Terrell, 1982), as dogmatic a position in one direction as that found in the other in Palmer (1922), who writes:

In opposition to the principle of accuracy, we are frequently told that 'It is only by making mistakes that we learn not to make them', and that 'Only by going into the water can we learn to swim'. These are cheap proverbs, and we may as easily coin others such as: 'It is by making mistakes that we form the habit of making them' or, 'He who has not learnt to swim will drown when thrown into deep water'.

The method of *trial and error*, to which we have already alluded, is in direct opposition to the principles of accuracy; it is the method of sink-or-swim, of die-or-survive, of flounder-and-grope-until-you-hit-on-the-right-way. To replace this method by something less cruel is the function of such things as guides, teachers, and pedagogic devices.   (Palmer, 1922: 65)

But, as we argue, we do not have to take an either/or position, and the comparisons made on both sides are neither of them exactly appropriate. Palmer, particularly, is failing to distinguish between *tokens* of the language, or usage, and the operation of those tokens within a value system, or use – see our discussion on teaching and learning in 4.2.

8   This is notwithstanding Stevick's claim that 'the distinction between adult "learning" and "acquisition" of language is potentially the most fruitful concept for language teachers that has come out of the linguistic sciences during my professional lifetime,' (Stevick, 1980: 270).

9   A few other examples, from Pickett's (1978) survey of the methods of successful learners: 'Method of learning: learn how the language is organised. The grammar, inflections, conjugations, declensions etc. etc., if possible from a good grammar book . . . ' (p. 61). 'I need always to have the grammar of a language laid out as a system for me. I cannot learn a language simply by induction . . . ' (p. 61). On vocabulary: 'Write all words on cards, and test endlessly, in *both* directions' (p. 68); 'I find that if I try to learn vocabulary I must concentrate on a word list and learn the items one by one with the front of my head' (p. 71).

10   Anyway, there is some indication that monitoring of speech may lead to less rather than more formal utterances (see Wolfson, 1976).

Chapter 4

1   This argument reflected similar preoccupations to those of Britton (1970: 248–62) in the mother-tongue situation, where he tries to relate the needs of young writers to the relationship between inner speech and writing hypothesised by Vygotsky (1962: 99–100).

2   Though traditional language-learning methods *can* be successful with some learners: cf. several entries in Pickett (1978) – note 9 to Chapter 3 above.

3   See, for example, Palmer (1922) in note 7 to Chapter 3 above.

4   'Mathetic' is 'language enabling the child to learn about his social and material environment, serving him in the construction of reality' (Halliday, 1975: 75).

5   cf. Rivers' 'Talking off the tops of their heads' (Rivers, 1972, esp. 28–9). Also Pickett's interesting observation (relevant to the starkness of the accuracy/fluency distinction as made here): 'All contributors mentioned *learning*

techniques e.g. memorising vocabulary, reading, doing written exercises etc., and all mentioned language *use* e.g. fluency, interference, dreaming, thinking in the language etc., but there seemed to be no middle ground between learning and using that could possibly be occupied by "practice" – a sort of game that you played with language acquired prior to using it in the real world' (Pickett, 1978: 30).

6   Thelen (1967: 33ff.) also illustrates how teacher–student relationships interact with general expectations about the role of teachers held in society at large.

7   Compare Birdwhistell (in Sebeok *et al.*, 1964: 188), 'I have a sense of horror that we are saying to ourselves that we have to learn to teach body motion or that we are going to have to learn to teach paralanguage. I think one of the things we need is some significant knowledge on how not to *prevent* children from learning these things' with Savignon (1972: 27–8); see also Sharwood Smith (1981) set against, say, Allwright (1977).

Chapter 5

1   Consider, for example, the implications for classroom relationships of the following statements from Dewey (1916):

On the intellectual side, the separation of 'mind' from direct occupation with things throws emphasis on *things* at the expense of *relations* or connections. It is altogether too common to separate perceptions and even ideas from judgements. (p. 143)

It is the nature of an experience to have implications which go far beyond what is at first consciously noted in it. Bringing these connections or implications to consciousness enhances the meaning of the experience. Any experience, however trivial in its first appearance, is capable of assuming an infinite richness of significance by extending its range of perceived connections. *Normal communication with others is the readiest way of effecting this development.* (p. 217; my italics)

Individual activity has sometimes been taken as meaning leaving a pupil to work by himself or alone. Relief from need of attending to what anyone else is doing is truly required to secure calm and concentration. Children, like grown persons, require a judicious amount of being let alone. But the time, place, and amount of such separate work is a matter of detail, not of principle. There is no inherent opposition between working with others and working as an individual. On the contrary, certain capacities of an individual are not brought out except under the stimulus of associating with others. That a child must work alone and not engage in group activities in order to be free and let his individuality develop, is a notion which measures individuality by spatial distance and makes a physical thing of it. (p. 302)

It would be possible to illustrate this tendency with many other quotations, but these will suffice to show that communication and interaction were concepts closely bound up with Dewey's epistemological position.

2   But Johnson and Johnson's work has nonetheless been used as a basis for language teaching – see page 94.

3   See, for example, Rivers (1972: 32–3):

Unfortunately, the emphasis on correct production at all times and the firm determination to create a learning situation where students would not make mistakes seems to have led to an impasse for many students. If we wish to facilitate the 'great leap' [towards what I have called fluency – CJB] . . . then a change of attitude towards mistakes during interaction practice is imperative . . . In interaction practice we are trying to develop an attitude of innovation and experimentation with the new language.

4   We might note the similarity (though it is not exact) between fluency activities and co-operative procedures as defined here; it is arguable that language use is frequently co-operative, and certainly accuracy work will be more suitable for competitive procedures.

5   See, for example, Allwright (1976: 177–8), where the exercise involves manipulation of pieces of Lego, or the emphasis of British Council films such as *Activity Days in Language Learning* (1977) and *Communication Games in a Language Programme* (1978). For a consideration of such activities which carefully relates them to wider syllabus objectives, see Rixon (1981).

6   It may sometimes be appropriate to encourage mistakes in order to assist students to resist the temptation to fall into them. This point has been made generally by Hamlyn (1978: 129):

It may sometimes be the case that getting into a wrong position is the best way of getting out of it in such a way as to ensure that we do not fall into the trap again, or the best way of making a leap forward where there might have been a crawl.

A view such as this throws light on the procedures of reading strategies such as those of Munby (1968), in which multiple-choice questions tempt students to fall into interpretation traps which are based on observed misreadings and misunderstandings. The process of discussing criteria for acceptance or rejection of particular answers is expected to assist the development of sound reading strategies.

Chapter 6

1   David Stern (personal communication) has suggested that translation should be added to the elements under 'communicative abilities'. He argues that in many bilingual situations, such as many parts of Canada, the ability to produce a more or less simultaneous translation in conversation may well be required of many learners. Certainly, there is no reason why such an ability should not be developed in school, but it is probably more helpful to regard translation as a particular need rather than one that should be specified in a chart like this, intended to apply to all circumstances. It is also an ability which must be secondary to the first, second, and possibly the fourth of those listed, for it depends on all these being developed to a certain extent.

2   For more sympathetic assessments, see Bancroft (1978), Stevick (1980: 229–59), O'Connell (1982), and, from a Soviet point of view, Leontiev (1981: 110–22).

3   See Tulving (1962) for relations between lists of words. Such tendencies to systematise are also observable in the selective, but sensible, recall of stories in the famous experiments of Bartlett (1932).

4   For a discussion of the origins of the concept of 'action research' and a criti-

cism of its value in language teaching, see Jarvis (1980). I use the term here with the meaning 'research which is motivated by a specific local problem and is designed only to resolve that problem in that setting'. But Prabhu's situation is beginning to move towards that of a later definition: 'The purpose of action research is to combine the research function with teacher growth in such qualities as objectivity, skill in research processes, habits of thinking, ability to work harmoniously with others, and professional spirit.' Both these definitions are cited in Jarvis (1980: 59).

5   Though Stevick does offer advice to general teachers in his latest book (Stevick, 1982), albeit with a specific warning about his own experience: 'Since I myself have never taught some types of class, this book lays no claim to being comprehensive' (p. 1).

Chapter 7

1   This distinction is discussed more fully in my contribution to Wilkins, Brumfit, and Paulston (1981).

2   This argument and design are compatible with a view widely held in the literature (for example, in Johnson, 1976), that communicative procedures are more important at post-elementary stages of language learning – though we are arguing here that they are important right from the very beginning. What is not explored in the literature, though, is the implication of this argument that the syllabus, if it is to facilitate learning most effectively, should not be based on time units, but on content or language specifications only. One of the major defects of almost all language syllabuses is the determination that a large body of linguistic content should be 'covered'. In practice, this usually means that it is presented – more or less – to everybody, but that few students have time to assimilate new material before they are exposed to the next chunk. Even if the material was carefully sequenced to be programmed logically and linearly (which it usually is not), the wish to incorporate more and more linguistic content would prevent effective learning for many learners. Our argument is that a limited system used flexibly will be more valuable than the unassimilated parts of an immense system presented rapidly and separately.

3   For the arguments that such lists lack theoretical motivation, see Davies (1981); Widdowson (1983).

4   See also Levine (1982) for a discussion of the relation between some similar activities for second-language learners and the mainstream curriculum.

5   Though we should note that many third-world countries achieve fluency partly through using a foreign language as the medium of instruction, thus coming close to the immersion model. For an example of recent attempts to relate English teaching to other subjects, see Grant and Ndanga (1980).

6   Strevens gives an account of possible linguistic models, in support of which cultural understanding will be necessary.

Notes

Chapter 8

1   For action research, see Chapter 6, note 4, above.

2   Blurred focus:

> A very poorly focussed colour slide is projected. It should be possible barely to make out blobs of colour. In pairs, students speculate about what they can see. The focus is then sharpened slightly. Students speculate again, changing their previous opinion if appropriate. The procedure continues until the slide is sharply focussed.

3   And indeed they have often been specifically recommended for foreign learners – see Ogden (1930); Quirk (1981).

4   This position is implied by Gary (1978) and other research cited there.

5   Under (iii) will be included issues like the degree of literary sophistication demanded as a necessary prelude to satisfactory reading of the work. An unsophisticated reader may find the parody in *Ulysses*, and a whole range of literary parallels in that work, so inaccessible as to make it unreadable – to give an extreme example. *The Rape of the Lock* is difficult to respond to without some appreciation of the tradition of which it is a burlesque. Under (iv) will be included the inaccessibility of imagery and reference within the work itself.

Appendix: Bangalore exercise (see page 104)

(Prabhu, 1982: Lesson 183: 26 August 1981)

The following dialogue is handed out and read aloud by two sets of students, each taking a part.

Suresh: Daddy, when will the train come?
Rajan: In about ten minutes. It is only 4.10 pm now.
Suresh: Will it leave the station at once?
Rajan: No Suresh, it will stop here for 10 minutes. It leaves Madras only at 4.30 pm.
Radha: Does it reach Hyderabad by 7.00 am?
Rajan: No, only at 8.30 am. We must have our breakfast in the train.
Suresh: How much did you pay for the tickets, Daddy?
Rajan: I paid Rs 360.00 for three first class tickets. When we come back from Hyderabad, we shall travel by second class.
Radha: Yes. A second-class ticket costs only Rs 50/–.
Suresh: Are we going to stay at Hotel Annapurna this time too, Mummy?
Radha: Yes dear, the rooms are very comfortable there.
Rajan: And the food is also good.
Radha: When do we come back to Madras?
Rajan: After a week. We will be back here at the Central Station on Saturday, the 22nd of August.
Suresh: Today is also a Saturday.Our school has holidays for a week from today.
Radha: There is the train! Suresh, take this bag. I'll take this suitcase. Daddy can take the bigger suitcase. We must find our compartment.

Pre-task: The teacher discusses with the class the following questions:

1   Who is Suresh?
2   What is his father's name?
3   Who is Radha?
4   Where are they now?
5   What is the name of the station?
6   What are they doing there?
7   Where are they going?
8   At what time does the train leave Madras?
9   How long does it take to reach Hyderabad?
10 Is it a night train or a day train?
11 Where will they stay in Hyderabad?
12 Will they have breakfast at Hotel Annapurna tomorrow?
13 Does Rajan like to stay at Annapurna? How do you know?
14 Why does Radha like Hotel Annapurna?

15 For how many days will they stay at Hyderabad?
16 On which day are they leaving Madras?
17 Will Suresh miss his classes?
18 What luggage do they have?
19 Are they rich? How do you know?
20 How much does a first class ticket cost?
21 How much will they spend for their return from Hyderabad to Madras?
22 The Hyderabad Express leaves Hyderabad at 4.00 pm. When does it reach Madras?
23 Last week Rajan went to Hyderabad. He travelled by second class both ways. How much did he spend on the train tickets?
24 Is this the first time that they are going to Hyderabad? How do you know?

Task: Pupils are asked to answer the following questions overnight.

Say whether the following statements are true or false; give reasons for your answers.
1 Mr Rajan always travels by first class.
2 There are no good hotels in Hyderabad.
3 The Rajans reached the station before the train arrived.
4 Radha can attend her friend's wedding at Hyderabad on 20th August.
5 Suresh was at Madras on Independence Day.

Comment: Pupils' performance, marked out of 10, was:

Marks	Pupils
9–10	9
7–8	10
5–6	3
3–4	0
1–2	1
	23

Pupils are now beginning to try to state reasons in their 'own words' instead of merely citing lines from the text.

Bibliography

Abercrombie, M.L.J. 1970, *Aims and Techniques in Group Teaching*, London, Society for Research into Higher Education.

AILA (Association Internationale de Linguistique Appliquée) (ed.) 1972, Proceedings of the Third International Congress of Applied Linguistics, Copenhagen, Heidelberg, Julius Groos Verlag.

Alatis, J., H. Altman and P. Alatis (eds.) 1981, *The Second Language Classroom: Directions for the 1980s*, New York, Oxford University Press.

Alexander, L.G. 1971, *Guided Composition in English Teaching*, London, Longman.

Allen, J.P.B. and S. Pit Corder (eds.) 1974, *The Edinburgh Course in Applied Linguistics*, Vol. 3, *Techniques in Applied Linguistics*, Oxford University Press.

Allwright, R.L. 1976, 'Putting cognitions on the map', *UCLA Workpapers*, Vol. X, June: 1–14.

1977, 'Language learning through communication practice', *ELT Documents* 76/3, London, The British Council: 2–14 (cited from Brumfit and Johnson, 1979).

1980, 'Turns, topics and tasks: patterns of participation in language learning and teaching', in Larsen-Freeman, 1980: 165–87.

Altman, Howard B. and C. Vaughan James (eds.) 1980, *Foreign Language Teaching: Meeting Individual Needs*, Oxford, Pergamon Press.

Altman, Howard B. and Robert L. Politzer (eds.) 1971, *Individualizing Foreign Language Instruction*, Rowley, Mass., Newbury House.

Andersen, Roger W. 1977, 'The impoverished state of cross-sectional morpheme acquisition/accuracy methodology', *Working Papers on Bilingualism*, 14, October: 47–82.

Andrews, J. 1975, *Say What You Mean in English*, London, Nelson.

Anthony, E.M. 1963, 'Approach, method and technique', *English Language Teaching*, XVII, 2: 63–7.

Apel, Karl-Otto 1976, 'The transcendental conception of language communication and the idea of a first philosophy', in Parret, 1976: 32–61.

Argyle, Michael, Adrian Furnham and Jean Ann Graham 1981, *Social Situations*, Cambridge University Press.

Asch, Solomon E. 1956, 'Studies of independence and conformity 1: a minority of one against a unanimous majority', *Psychology Monographs, General and Applied*, 70, 9, Whole no. 416.

Austin, J.L. 1962, *How to Do Things with Words*, Oxford University Press.

Axtell, James L. 1968. *The Educational Writings of John Locke*, Cambridge University Press.

Bamgbose, A. (ed.) 1976, *Mother Tongue Education: the West African Experience*, London, Hodder and Stoughton, and Paris, UNESCO.

Bibliography

Bancroft, W. Jane 1978, 'The Lozanov method and its American adaptations', *Modern Language Journal*, 62, 4: 167–74.

Barnes, Douglas 1969, 'Language in the secondary classroom', in Barnes, Britton and Rosen, 1969: 9–77.

  1976, *From Communication to Curriculum*, Harmondsworth, Penguin.

Barnes, Douglas, James Britton and Harold Rosen 1969, *Language, the Learner and the School*, Harmondsworth, Penguin.

Bartlett, F.C. 1932, *Remembering: a Study in Experimental and Social Psychology*, Cambridge University Press.

Bartley, Diana E. 1971, *Soviet Approaches to Bilingual Education*, Philadelphia, Center for Curriculum Development.

Bayley, John 1966, *Tolstoy and the Novel*, London, Chatto and Windus.

Berger, Charles R. 1979, 'Beyond initial interaction: uncertainty, understanding, and the development of interpersonal relationships', in Giles and St Clair, 1979: 122–44.

Berger, P.L. and T. Luckman 1966, *The Social Construction of Reality*, Garden City, NJ, Doubleday.

Berlin, Isaiah 1980, *Against the Current: Essays in the History of Ideas*, ed. Henry Hardy, New York, The Viking Press.

Bernstein, Basil 1969, 'A critique of the concept of compensatory education', in Bernstein, 1971: 190–201.

  1971, *Class, Codes and Control*, Vol. 1, *Theoretical Studies towards a Sociology of Language*, London, Routledge and Kegan Paul.

Bialystok, E. 1978, 'A theoretical model of second language learning', *Language Learning* 28, 1, June: 69–84.

Bialystok, E. and M. Fröhlich 1977, 'Aspects of second language learning in classroom settings', *Working Papers on Bilingualism* 13, May: 1–26.

Bibeau, Gilles 1983, 'La théorie du moniteur de Krashen: aspects critiques', *Bulletin of the CAAL*, Spring: 99–123.

Blatchford, Charles H. and Jacquelyn Schachter (eds.) 1978, *On TESOL '78: EFL Policies, Programs, Practice*, Washington DC, TESOL.

Bloom, B.S. 1956, *Taxonomy of Educational Objectives*, New York, McKay.

Bourhis, R.Y. and Howard Giles 1977, 'The language of intergroup distinctiveness', in Giles, 1977: 119–35.

Bourhis, R.Y., Howard Giles, Jacques P. Leyens and Henri Tajfel 1979, 'Psycholinguistic distinctiveness: language divergence in Belgium', in Giles and St Clair, 1979: 158–85.

Bramley, Wyn 1979, *Group Tutoring, Concepts and Case Studies*, London, Kogan Page.

Breen, Michael P. and Christopher N. Candlin 1980, 'The essentials of a communicative curriculum in language teaching', *Applied Linguistics* 1, 2, Summer: 89–112.

Brière, E.J. 1978, 'Variables affecting native Mexican children's learning Spanish as a second language', *Language Learning* 28, 1, June: 159–74.

Bright, J.A. and G.P. McGregor 1970, *Teaching English as a Second Language*, London, Longman.

Britton, J. 1970, *Language and Learning*, London, Allen Lane, The Penguin Press.

Bromley, D.B. 1966, *The Psychology of Human Ageing*, Harmondsworth, Penguin.

Brophy, Jese E. and Thomas L. Good 1974, *Teacher–Student Relationships: Causes and Consequences*, New York, Holt Rinehart and Winston.

Broughton, Geoffrey, Christopher Brumfit, Roger Flavell, Peter Hill and Anita Pincas 1978, *Teaching English as a Foreign Language*, London, Routledge and Kegan Paul.

Brown, H. Douglas 1981, 'Affective factors in second language learning', in Alatis, Altman and Alatis, 1981: 113–29.

Brown, J.D. 1981, 'Newly placed students versus continuing students: comparing proficiency', in Fisher, Clarke and Schachter, 1981: 111–19.

Brown, P. and S. Levinson 1978, 'Universals in language usage', in Goody, 1978: 56–289.

Brown, Roger 1973, *A First Language: the Early Stages*, London, Allen and Unwin.

Brumfit, C.J. 1971, 'Second language teaching in the secondary school – some principles', *Bulletin of the Language Association of Tanzania*, 3, 2, April: 18–26 (cited from Brumfit, 1980: 28–38).

1979, 'Accuracy and fluency as polarities in foreign language teaching materials and methodology', *Bulletin CILA*, 29: 89–99.

1980, *Problems and Principles in English Teaching*, Oxford, Pergamon Press.

(ed.) 1982, *English for International Communication*, Oxford, Pergamon Press.

Brumfit, C.J. and K. Johnson (eds.) 1979, *The Communicative Approach to Language Teaching*, Oxford University Press.

Bruner, Jerome S. 1960, *The Process of Education*, Cambridge, Mass., Harvard University Press.

Burke, Peter 1981, 'Languages and anti languages in early modern Italy', *History Workshop* 11, Spring: 24–32.

Burt, Marina K. and Heidi C. Dulay (eds.) 1975, *On TESOL '75: New Directions in Language Learning, Teaching, and Bilingual Education*, Washington DC, TESOL.

Byrne, Donn 1979, *Teaching Writing Skills*, London, Longman.

Canale, Michael and Merrill Swain 1980, 'Theoretical bases of communicative approaches to second language teaching and testing', *Applied Linguistics* 1, 1, Spring: 1–47.

Carroll, Brendan J. 1980, *Testing Communicative Performance*, Oxford, Pergamon Press.

Chihara, T. and J.W. Oller Jr 1978, 'Attitudes and attained proficiency in EFL: a sociolinguistic study of adult Japanese speakers', *Language Learning* 28, 1, June: 55–68.

Chomsky, Noam 1957, *Syntactic Structures*, The Hague, Mouton.

1965, *Aspects of the Theory of Syntax*, Cambridge, Mass., MIT Press.

1980, *Rules and Representations*, New York, Columbia University Press.

Christopherson, Paul 1972, *Second-Language Learning; Myth and Reality*, Harmondsworth, Penguin.

Ciotti, Marianne C. 1969, 'A conceptual framework for small-group instruction in high school', *Foreign Language Annuals* 3, 1, October: 75–89.

Clark, Eve V. 1979, *The Ontogenesis of Meaning*, Wiesbaden, Athenaion.

Clark, Eve V. and C.J. Sengul 1978, 'Strategies in the acquisition of deixis', *Journal of Child Language* 5: 457–75.

Cole, P. and J. Morgan (eds.) 1975, *Syntax and Semantics*, Vol. 3, *Speech Acts*, New York, Academic Press.

Colodny, Robert G. (ed.) 1962, *Frontiers of Science and Philosophy*, University of Pittsburgh Press.

Cooper, Cary L. 1979, *Learning from Others in Groups*, London, Associated Business Press.

Cooper, Robert L. 1968, 'An elaborated language testing model', *Language Learning*, Special Issue no. 3: 57–72.

Corder, S. Pit 1973, *Introducing Applied Linguistics*, Harmondsworth, Penguin.
    1975, 'Error analysis, interlanguage and second language acquisition', *Language Teaching and Linguistics Abstracts* 8, 4, October: 201–18.
    1981, *Error Analysis and Interlanguage*, Oxford University Press.

Cortis, Gerald 1977, *The Social Context of Teaching*, London, Open Books.

Coulthard, R.M. 1977, *An Introduction to Discourse Analysis*, London, Longman.

Crawford-Lange, Linda M. 1982, 'Curricular alternatives for second-language learning', in Higgs, 1982: 81–112.

Cross, David 1980, 'Personalized language learning', in Altman and James, 1980: 111–24.

Crymes, Ruth 1980, 'Current trends in ESL instruction', *TESOL Newsletter* XIV, 4, August: 1–4 and 18.

Crystal, D. 1971, 'Stylistics, fluency and language teaching', in *Interdisciplinary Approaches to Language*, *CILT Reports and Papers* 6, London, Centre for Information on Language Teaching: 34–52.

Cummins, J. 1979, 'Linguistic interdependence and the educational development of bilingual children', *Review of Educational Research* 49, 2, Spring: 222–51.

Dakin, J., B. Tiffen and H.G. Widdowson 1968, *Language in Education*, Oxford University Press.

Davies, Alan 1981, Review of Munby, *Communicative Syllabus Design*, *TESOL Quarterly* 15, 3, September: 332–6.

Day, Richard R. 1982, 'Children's attitudes towards language', in Ryan and Giles, 1982: 116–31.

De Houwer, Annick 1982, 'Second language acquisition: a survey of recent literature', *ITL: A Review of Applied Linguistics* 55: 39–68.

De Quincey, Thomas 1822, *Confessions of an English Opium Eater*, London, Dent, Everyman (Everyman edn, 1907).

Dewey, John 1916, *Democracy and Education*, New York, Macmillan.

Dilthey, W. 1976, *Selected Writings*, ed. and trans. from German by H.P. Rickman, Cambridge University Press.

Dixon, John 1967, *Growth through English*, Oxford University Press.

Dore, J. 1974, 'A pragmatic description of early language development', *Journal of Psycholinguistic Research* 3, 4, October: 343–50.

Dykstra, Gerald, Richard Port and Antoinette Port 1968, *Ananse Tales*, New York, Teachers College Columbia.

Easton, David 1965, *A Framework for Political Analysis*, Englewood Cliffs, NJ, Prentice-Hall.

Ervin-Tripp, S. 1974, 'Is second language learning like the first?' *TESOL Quarterly* 8, 2: 111–27.

Escher, Erwin 1928, 'The Direct Method of Studying Foreign Languages: a

Contribution to the History of its Sources and Development', unpublished Ph.D. thesis, University of Chicago.

Fathman, A. 1975, 'The relationship between age and second language productive ability', *Language Learning* 25, 2, December: 245–53.

1976, 'Variables affecting the successful learning of English as a second language', *TESOL Quarterly* 10, 4, December: 433–41.

Ferguson, Nicola 1977, 'Simultaneous speech, interruptions, and dominance', *British Journal of Social and Clinical Psychology* 16, 4, November: 295–302.

Feyerabend, Paul 1975, *Against Method*, London, Verso.

Fillmore, Charles J. 1979, 'On fluency', in Fillmore, Kempler and Wang, 1979: 85–101.

Fillmore, Charles J., Daniel Kempler and William S.-Y. Wang (eds.) 1979, *Individual Differences in Language Ability and Language Behavior*, New York, Academic Press.

Fillmore, Lily Wong 1979, 'Individual differences in second language acquisition', in Fillmore, Kempler and Wang, 1979: 203–28.

Fisher, J.C., M.A. Clarke and J. Schachter (eds.) 1981, *On TESOL '80*, Washington DC, TESOL.

Fishman, J. (ed.) 1968, *Readings in the Sociology of Language*, The Hague, Mouton.

Flynn, Elizabeth W. and John La Faso 1972, *Group Discussion as Learning Process*, New York, Paulist Press.

Forrester, J. 1968, *Teaching without Lecturing*, Oxford University Press.

Freedman, Elaine S. 1971, 'The road from Pennsylvania – where next in language teaching experimentation?' *Audio-Visual Language Journal*, IX, 1, Spring: 33–8.

1976, 'Experimentation into foreign language teaching methodology', *System*, 4, 1, January: 12–28.

1982, 'Experimentation into foreign language teaching methodology: the research findings', *System*, 10, 2: 119–33.

Freire, Paulo 1971, *Pedagogy of the Oppressed*, trans. from Portuguese by Myra Bergman Ramos, New York, Herder and Herder (original Portuguese, 1968).

1981, 'The people speak their word: learning to read and write in São Tomé and Principe', *Harvard Educational Review* 51, 1, February: 27–30.

French, Patrice L. (ed.) 1979, *The Development of Meaning*, Hiroshima, Bunka Hyoron.

Gahagan, Judy 1975, *Interpersonal and Group Behaviour*, London, Methuen.

Gardner, R.C. 1979, 'Social psychological aspects of second language acquisition', in Giles and St Clair, 1979: 193–220.

Gary, Judith Olmsted 1978, 'Why speak if you don't need to? The case for a listening approach to beginning foreign language learning', in Ritchie, 1978: 185–99.

Gary, Norman and Judith Olmsted Gary 1982, 'Packaging comprehension materials: towards effective language instruction in difficult circumstances', *System*, 10, 1: 61–9.

Gattegno, Caleb 1972, *Teaching Foreign Languages in Schools: The Silent Way*, 2nd edn, New York, Educational Solutions Inc. (1st edn, 1963).

Giddens, A. 1982, 'Reasons to believe', *Times Higher Education Supplement*, 11 June 1982: 14–15.

Giles, H. (ed.) 1977, *Language, Ethnicity and Intergroup Relations*, London, Academic Press.

Giles, H. and Jane L. Byrne 1982, 'An intergroup approach to second language acquisition', *Journal of Multilingual and Multicultural Development* 3, 1: 17–40.

Giles, H. and Robert St Clair (eds.) 1979, *Language and Social Psychology*, Oxford, Basil Blackwell.

Gingras, Rosario C. (ed.) 1978, *Second-Language Acquisition and Foreign Language Teaching*, Arlington, Va., Center for Applied Linguistics.

Gleason, Jean B. and S. Weintraub 1976, 'The acquisition of routines in child language', *Language in Society* 5, 2, August: 129–36.

Goffman, E. 1959, *The Presentation of Self in Everyday Life*, London, Allen Lane, The Penguin Press.

1961, *Encounters*, Harmondsworth, Penguin.

1967, *Interaction Ritual*, New York, Doubleday.

Goodman, Kenneth S. 1969, 'Analysis of oral reading miscues: applied psycholinguistics', *Reading Research Quarterly* 5, 1: 9–30.

Goody, E.N. (ed.) 1978, *Questions and Politeness: Strategies in Social Interaction*, Cambridge University Press.

Gordon, J.C.B. 1978, *The Reception of Bernstein's Sociolinguistic Theory among Primary School Teachers*, UEA Papers in Linguistics, Supplement no. 1, October, Norwich, University of East Anglia.

Gorman, T.P. (ed.) 1970, *Language in Education in Eastern Africa*, Nairobi, Oxford University Press.

Grant, N.J.H. and H.J. Ndanga 1980, *English for Zimbabwe*, Book I, Harare, Longman.

Greenfield, P.M. and J. Smith 1976, *The Structure of Communication in Early Language Development*, New York, Academic Press.

Grice, H. 1975, 'Logic and conversation', in Cole and Morgan, 1975: 41–58.

Gumperz, J. and D.Hymes (eds.) 1972, *Directions in Sociolinguistics: the Ethnography of Communication*, New York, Holt Rinehart and Winston.

Gustafson, James P., Lowell Cooper, Nancy Coalter Lathrop, Karin Ringler, Fredric A. Seldin and Marina Kahn Wright 1981, 'Co-operative and clashing interests in small groups', *Human Relations* 34, 4, April: 315–39.

Habermas, J. 1970, 'On systematically distorted communication', *Inquiry* 13, 3, Autumn: 205–18 (also in H.P. Dreitzel (ed.) 1970, *Recent Sociology* no. 2, *Patterns of Communicative Behavior*, New York, Macmillan, under the title: 'Towards a theory of communicative competence').

Hale, T. and E. Budar 1970, 'Are TESOL classes the only answer?' *Modern Language Journal* 54, 7, November: 487–92.

Halliday, M.A.K. 1970, 'Language structure and language function', in Lyons, 1970: 140–65.

1973, *Explorations in the Functions of Language*, London, Edward Arnold.

1975, *Learning How to Mean*, London, Edward Arnold.

1976, ' "The teacher taught the student English": an essay in applied linguistics', *Second LACUS Forum*, ed. Peter A. Reich, Columbia, S. Carolina, Hornbeam Press: 344–9.

1978, *Language as Social Semiotic*, London, Edward Arnold.

Hamlyn, D.W. 1978, *Experience and the Growth of Understanding*, London, Routledge and Kegan Paul.

Handy, Charles B. 1976, *Understanding Organizations*, Harmondsworth, Penguin.
Hatch, Evelyn Marcussen (ed.) 1978, *Second Language Acquisition*, Rowley, Mass., Newbury House.
Hatch, Evelyn Marcussen and M. Long 1980, 'Discourse analysis, what's that?' in Larsen-Freeman, 1980: 1–40.
Hawkes, Terence 1977, *Structuralism and Semiotics*, London, Methuen.
Hempel, Carl G. 1962, 'Explanation in science and in history', in Colodny, 1962: 7–33.
Higgs, Theodore V. (ed.) 1982, *Curriculum, Competence, and the Foreign Language Teacher*, Skokie, Ill., National Textbook Company in conjunction with ACTFL.
Hinde, R.A. (ed.) 1972, *Non-verbal Communication*, Cambridge University Press.
1979, *Towards Understanding Relationships*, London, Academic Press.
Hirst, Paul 1974, *Knowledge and the Curriculum*, London, Routledge and Kegan Paul.
Hoetker, James 1975, 'Researching drama: an American view', in Stephenson and Vincent, 1975: 80–93.
Holden, Susan (ed.) 1977, *English for Specific Purposes*, London, Modern English Publications.
Hornby, A.S. 1955, 'In the classroom 1: using the group in oral work', *English Language Teaching*, 10, 1: 31–2.
Hornby, Peter A. 1980, 'Achieving second language fluency through immersion education', *Foreign Language Annals* 13, 2, April: 107–13.
Howatt, Anthony 1974, 'The background to course design', in Allen and Corder, 1974: 1–23.
1984, *A History of English Language Teaching*, Oxford University Press.
Huang, J. and E. Hatch 1978, 'A Chinese child's acquisition of English', in Hatch, 1978: 118–31.
Hudson, Liam 1968, *Frames of Mind*, London, Methuen.
1972, *The Cult of the Fact*, London, Jonathan Cape.
Hudson, R.A. 1980, *Sociolinguistics*, Cambridge University Press.
1981, 'Some issues on which linguists can agree', *Journal of Linguistics* 17, 2: 333–43.
Humboldt, W. von 1903–1936, *Gesammelte Schriften*, ed. Albert Leitzmann, 17 vols., Berlin, Prussian Academy of Sciences (cited from various secondary sources indicated in the text).
Hymes, D. 1964, 'Directions in (ethno-)linguistic theory', *American Anthropologist*, Special publication: *Transcultural Studies in Cognition*, ed. A. Kimball Romney and Roy Goodwin D'Andrade, 66, 3, Part 2: 6–56.
1967, 'Models of the interaction of language and social setting', *Journal of Social Issues* 23, 2: 8–28.
1968, 'The ethnography of speaking', in Fishman, 1968: 99–138.
1971, *On Communicative Competence*, Philadelphia, University of Pennsylvania Press (extensively extracted in Pride and Holmes, 1972, and Brumfit and Johnson, 1979: 5–24, from which cited).
Ingram, D. 1978, 'Sensorimotor intelligence and language development', in Lock, 1978: 261–90.
Ions, Edmund 1977, *Against Behaviouralism: a Critique of Behavioural Science*, Oxford, Basil Blackwell.

Bibliography

Isaacs, R.H. (ed.) 1968, *Learning through Language: Teachers' Book*, Dar es Salaam, Tanzania Publishing House.

Jackson, P.W. 1968, *Life in Classrooms*, New York, Holt Rinehart and Winston.

Jakobovits, Leon A. 1970, 'Prolegomena to a theory of communicative competence', in Lugton, 1970: 1–39.

Jakobovits, Leon A. and Barbara Gordon 1974, *The Context of Foreign Language Teaching*, Rowley, Mass., Newbury House.

James, Juliane 1980, 'Learner variation: the monitor model and language learning strategies', *Interlanguage Studies Bulletin 5*, 2, Autumn: 99–111.

Jarvis, Gilbert A. 1980, 'Action research versus needed research for the 1980's', in *Proceedings of the National Conference on Professional Priorities*, November 1980, Boston, ACTFL: 59–63.

Jeffcoate, Robert 1979, *Positive Image*, London, Writers and Readers Publishing Co-operative.

Johnson, David W. and Roger T. Johnson 1975, *Learning Together and Alone*, Englewood Cliffs, NJ, Prentice-Hall.

Johnson, Keith 1976, 'The production of functional materials and their integration within existing language-teaching programmes', *ELT Documents* 76/1: 16–25.

    1981, 'Some background, some key terms and some definitions', in Johnson and Morrow, 1981: 1–12.

    1982, *Communicative Syllabus Design and Methodology*, Oxford, Pergamon Press.

Johnson, Keith and Keith Morrow (eds.) 1981, *Communication in the Classroom*, London, Longman.

Jolly, David and Patrick Early 1974, 'Group work in English language teaching', mimeo, The British Council, Belgrade, May.

Jones, Leo 1977, *Functions of English*, Cambridge University Press.

Jones, Richard M. 1968, *Fantasy and Feeling in Education*, New York, Harper and Row.

Jupp, T.C. and John Milne 1968, *A Guided Course in English Composition*, London, Heinemann.

    1972, *Guided Paragraph Writing*, London, Heinemann.

Kaye, Barrington and Irving Rogers 1968, *Group Work in Secondary Schools*, Oxford University Press.

Keating, R.F. 1963, *A Study of the Effectiveness of Language Laboratories*, New York, Teachers College Columbia.

Kelly, Louis G. 1969, *25 Centuries of Language Teaching*, Rowley, Mass., Newbury House.

Kilpatrick, William Heard 1940, *Group Education for a Democracy*, New York, Association Press.

Kinsella, V. (ed.) 1978, *Language Teaching and Linguistics: Surveys*, Cambridge University Press.

Koestler, Arthur 1964, *The Act of Creation*, London, Hutchinson.

Krashen, Stephen D. 1976, 'Formal and informal linguistic environments in language learning and language acquisition', *TESOL Quarterly* 10, 2, June: 157–68.

    1978, 'The monitor model for second language acquisition', in Gingras, 1978: 1–26.

1979, 'A response to McLaughlin "The monitor model: some methodological considerations" ', *Language Learning* 29, 1, June: 151–67.

1981a, *Second Language Acquisition and Second Language Learning*, Oxford, Pergamon Press.

1981b, 'Effective second language acquisition: insights from research', in Alatis, Altman and Alatis, 1981: 95–109.

1982, *Principles and Practice in Second Language Acquisition*, Oxford, Pergamon Press.

Krashen, Stephen D., C. Jones, S. Zelinski and C. Usprich 1978, 'How important is instruction?' *English Language Teaching Journal*, 32, 4, July: 257–61.

Kuhn, Thomas S. 1962, 2nd edn 1970, *The Structure of Scientific Revolutions*, University of Chicago Press.

Labov, W. 1969, 'The logic of non-standard English', *Georgetown Monographs on Language and Linguistics*, Vol. 22: 1–31.

1972, *Sociolinguistic Patterns*, Philadelphia, University of Pennsylvania Press.

Lakatos, Imre 1970, 'Falsification and the methodology of scientific research programmes', in Lakatos and Musgrave, 1970: 91–196.

Lakatos, Imre and Alan Musgrave (eds.) 1970, *Criticism and the Growth of Knowledge*, Cambridge University Press.

Langford, G. 1968, *Philosophy and Education*, London, Macmillan.

Larsen-Freeman, Diane E. 1975, 'The acquisition of grammatical morphemes by adult ESL students', *TESOL Quarterly* 9, 4, December: 409–19.

(ed.) 1980, *Discourse Analysis in Second Language Research*, Rowley, Mass., Newbury House.

Lawler, J. and L. Selinker 1971, 'On paradoxes, rules and research in second language learning', *Language Learning* 21, 1, June: 27–43.

Lee, W.R. 1965, *Language Teaching Games and Contests*, Oxford University Press.

Leeson, Richard 1975, *Fluency and Language Teaching*, London, Longman.

Leontiev, Alexei A. 1981, *Psychology and the Language Learning Process* (anonymously trans. from undated Russian text), Oxford, Pergamon Press.

Leopold, W.F. 1972, *Bibliography of Child Language*, updated by D. Slobin, Bloomington, Indiana University Press (original publication, 1952, Evanston, Ill., Northwestern University Press).

Le Page, R. 1975, 'Sociolinguistics and the problem of "competence" ', *Language Teaching and Linguistics Abstracts*, 8, 3, July: 137–56 (reprinted in Kinsella, 1978: 39–59).

Levine, Josie 1982, 'Second language learning and mainstream curriculum: learning as we go', paper for conference on 'The Practice of Intercultural Education', Nijenrode, Breukelen, The Netherlands, mimeo, University of London Institute of Education.

Lewin, Kurt, Ronald Lippitt and Ralph K. White 1939, 'Patterns of aggressive behavior in experimentally created "social climates" ', *Journal of Social Psychology* 10, 2, May: 271–99.

Lewis, E. Glyn 1977, 'Bilingualism and bilingual education – the ancient world to the renaissance', in Spolsky and Cooper, 1977: 22–93.

Lock, A.J. (ed.) 1978, *Action, Gesture, and Symbol: The Emergence of Language*, New York, Academic Press.

1980, *The Guided Reinvention of Language*, London, Academic Press.

Locke, John 1693, *Some Thoughts Concerning Education*, London, Awnsham and John Churchill (cited from Axtell, 1968).

Long, Michael H. 1975, 'Group work and communicative competence in the ESOL classroom', in Burt and Dulay, 1975: 217–23.

1982, 'Does second language instruction make a difference?', paper delivered at TESOL Convention, Honolulu, May, mimeo.

Lozanov, Georgi 1978, *Suggestology and Outlines of Suggestopedy*, trans. from Bulgarian by Marjorie Hall-Pozharlieva and Krassimira Pashmakova, London, Gordon and Breach (original edn, 1971, Nauki i Izkustvi, Sofia).

Lugton, Robert C. (ed.) 1970, *English as a Second Language: Current Issues*, Philadelphia, Center for Curriculum Development.

Lyons, John (ed.) 1970, *New Horizons in Linguistics*, Harmondsworth, Penguin.

1972, 'Human language', in Hinde, 1972: 49–85.

1977, *Semantics*, 2 vols., Cambridge University Press.

1981, *Language and Linguistics*, Cambridge University Press.

Lyons, John and R.J. Wales (eds.) 1966, *Psycholinguistics Papers*, Edinburgh University Press.

McAdam, B. 1970, 'The English medium scheme in Zambia', in Gorman, 1970: 37–50.

Mackay, R. and A. Mountford (eds.) 1978, *English for Specific Purposes*, London, Longman.

Mackey, W.F. 1965, *Language Teaching Analysis*, London, Longman.

McLaughlin, Barry 1978a, *Second Language Acquisition in Childhood*, Hillsdale, NJ, Lawrence Erlbaum Associates.

1978b, 'The monitor model: some methodological considerations', *Language Learning* 28, 2, December: 309–32.

1980, 'Theory and research in second language learning: an emerging paradigm', *Language Learning* 30, 2, December: 331–50.

Macnamara, J. (ed.) 1977, *Language Learning and Thought*, New York, Academic Press.

Magee, Bryan 1973, *Popper*, London, Collins, Fontana.

Maley, Alan 1981, 'Games and problem solving', in Johnson and Morrow, 1981: 137–48.

Maley, Alan and Alan Duff 1978, *Drama Techniques in Language Learning*, Cambridge University Press (2nd edn 1982).

Maples, Mary F. 1979, 'A humanistic education: basic ingredients', *The Humanistic Educator* 17, 3, March: 107–10.

Marcel, Claude 1853, *Language as a Means of Mental Culture and International Communication: or the Manual of the Teacher and Learner of Languages*, 2 vols., London, Chapman and Hall.

Martin, G.M.St 1980, 'English language acquisition: the effects of living with an American family', *TESOL Quarterly* 14, 3, September: 388–90.

Mason, C. 1971, 'The relevance of intensive training in English as a foreign language for university students', *Language Learning* 21, 2, December: 197–204.

Mead, Margaret 1964, 'Discussion session on language teaching', in Sebeok, Hayes and Bateson, 1964: 189.

Medawar, Peter 1967, *The Art of the Soluble*, London, Methuen.

Milgram, S. 1963, 'Behavioral study of obedience', *Journal of Abnormal and Social Psychology* 67, 4, October: 371–8.

1965, 'Liberating effects pressure', *Journal of Personality and Social Psychology* 1, 2, February: 127–34.

Mill, John Stuart 1843, *A System of Logic*, London, Longmans Green.

Mitchell, Rosamond, Brian Parkinson and Richard Johnstone 1981, *The Foreign Language Classroom: an Observational Study*, Stirling Educational Monographs no. 9, Department of Education, University of Stirling.

Moody, K.W. 1966, *Written English under Control*, Ibadan, Oxford University Press.

Moore, T.E. (ed.) 1973, *Cognitive Development and the Acquisition of Language*, New York, Academic Press.

Morrow, Keith 1977, *Techniques of Evaluation for a Notional Syllabus*, London, Royal Society of Arts.

1981, 'Principles of communicative methodology', in Johnson and Morrow, 1981: 59–66.

Munby, John 1968, *Read and Think*, London, Longman.

1978, *Communicative Syllabus Design*, Cambridge University Press.

Naiman, N., M. Fröhlich, H.H. Stern and A. Todesco 1978, *The Good Language Learner*, Research in Education Series no. 7, Toronto, Ontario Institute for Studies in Education.

Ochsner, Robert 1979, 'A poetics of second-language acquisition', *Language Learning* 29, 1: 53–80.

O'Connell, Peter 1982, 'Suggestopedy and the adult language learner', *ELT Documents* 113: 110–17.

Ogden, C.K. 1930, *Basic English*, London, Kegan Paul Trench Trubner.

Olson, David R. 1977, 'From utterance to text: the bias of language in speech and writing', *Harvard Educational Review*, 47, 3, August: 257–81.

Palmer, H.E. 1922, *The Principles of Language Study*, London, Harrap (cited from 1964 reprint, Oxford University Press).

Parker, J. Cecil and Louis J. Rubin 1966, *Process as Content*, Chicago, Rand McNally.

Parret, Herman (ed.) 1976, *History of Linguistic Thought and Contemporary Linguistics*, Berlin, Walter de Gruyter.

Pickett, G.D. 1978, *The Foreign Language Learning Process*, London, The British Council.

Polyani, Michael 1958, *Personal Knowledge: Towards a Post-Critical Philosophy*, London, Routledge and Kegan Paul.

Pompa, Leon (ed.) 1981, *Vico: Selected Writings*, Cambridge University Press.

Popper, Karl 1934, *Logik der Forschung*, Vienna, Julius Springer Verlag (dated 1935; cited from English translation by Karl Popper, *The Logic of Scientific Discovery*, London, Hutchinson, 1959).

1945, *The Open Society and its Enemies*, 2 vols., London, Routledge and Kegan Paul (cited from 5th edn, 1966).

1957, *The Poverty of Historicism*, London, Routledge and Kegan Paul.

1963, *Conjectures and Refutations*, London, Routledge and Kegan Paul.

1972, *Objective Knowledge*, Oxford University Press.

Popper, Karl and John C. Eccles 1977, *The Self and its Brain*, New York, Springer International.

Postovsky, V.A. 1974, 'Effects of delay in oral practice at the beginning of second language learning', *Modern Language Journal* LVIII, 5–6, September–October: 229–39.

Prabhu, N.S. 1982, 'The communicational teaching project, South India', mimeo, Madras, The British Council.

Pride, J.B. and Janet Holmes (eds.) 1972, *Sociolinguistics*, Harmondsworth, Penguin.

Quintilian 1920, *Institutio Oratoria*, 4 vols., ed. H.E. Butler, Loeb Library, London, Heinemann (written c. AD 90).

Quirk, Randolph 1981, 'International communication and the concept of nuclear English', in L. Smith, 1981: 151–65.

Ravich, R.A. and Wyden, B. 1974, *Predictable Pairings: the Structure of Human Atoms*, New York, Peter H. Wyden.

Reich, Peter A. (ed.) 1976, *The Second LACUS Forum*, Columbia, S. Carolina, Hornbeam Press.

Richterich, R. 1972, *A Model for the Definition of Language Needs of Adults Learning a Modern Language*, Strasbourg, Council of Europe.

Ringler, N.M., J.H. Kennell, R. Jarvella, B.J. Navojosky and M.H. Klaus 1975, 'Mother-to-child speech at two years: effects of early postnatal contact', *Journal of Pediatrics*, 86: 141.

Ritchie, William C. (ed.) 1978, *Second Language Acquisition Research*, New York, Academic Press.

Rivers, Wilga M. 1968, *Teaching Foreign Language Skills*, Chicago University Press.

1972, *Speaking in Many Tongues*, Rowley, Mass., Newbury House.

1979, 'Learning a sixth language: an adult learner's daily diary', *Canadian Modern Language Review* 36, 1, October: 67–82.

1980, 'A word about new methods', *English Teaching Forum* XVIII, 1, January, Editorial, inside cover.

Rixon, Shelagh 1981, *How to Use Games in Language Teaching*, London, Macmillan.

Robinson, Pauline 1980, *English for Specific Purposes*, Oxford, Pergamon Press.

Rogers, Carl 1969, *Freedom to Learn*, Columbus, Ohio, Merrill.

Rosansky, Ellen J. 1976, 'Methods and morphemes in second language acquisition research', *Language Learning* 26, 2, December: 409–25.

Rosenbaum, Peter S. 1973, *Peer-Mediated Instruction*, New York, Teachers College Press.

Rowlands, David (ed.) 1972, *Group-work in Modern Languages*, University of York.

Rubin, Louis J. (ed.) 1973, *Facts and Feelings in the Classroom*, New York, Walker and Co.

Ryan, Ellen Bouchard and Howard Giles (eds.) 1982, *Attitudes Towards Language Variation: Social and Applied Contexts*, London, Edward Arnold.

Sacks, H. 1972, 'On the analyzability of stories by children', in Gumperz and Hymes, 1972: 325–45.

Sacks, H., E. Schegloff and G. Jefferson 1974, 'A simplest systematics for the organization of turn-taking for conversation', *Language* 50, 4: 696–735.

Sajavaara, Kari 1978, 'The monitor model and monitoring in foreign language speech communication', in Gingras, 1978: 51–67.

1980, 'Psycholinguistic models, second language acquisition, and contrastive analysis', mimeo, University of Jyväskylä.

Sands, M.K. 1981, 'Group work: time for re-evaluation?' *Educational Studies* 7, 2: 77–86.

Saussure, F. de 1916, *Cours de Linguistique Générale*, Paris, Payot.

Savignon, Sandra J. 1972, *Communicative Competence: an Experiment in Foreign Language Teaching*, Philadelphia, Center for Curriculum Development.

    1981, 'A letter to my Spanish teacher', *Canadian Modern Languages Review* 37, 4, May: 746–50.

Scheffler, I. 1960, *The Language of Education*, Illinois, Charles C. Thomas.

Schegloff, E. 1968, 'Sequencing in conversational openings', *American Anthropologist* 70: 1075–95.

    1972, 'Notes on a conversational practice: formulating place', in Sudnow, 1972: 75–119.

Schein, Edgar H. 1965, *Organizational Psychology*, Englewood Cliffs, NJ, Prentice-Hall.

Scherer, G.A.C. and M. Wertheimer 1964, *A Psycholinguistic Experiment in Foreign Language Teaching*, New York, McGraw-Hill.

Schmidt, Richard W. and Jack C. Richards 1980, 'Speech acts and second language learning', *Applied Linguistics* I, 2, Summer: 129–57.

Schmidt, Siegfried J. 1976, 'German philosophy of language in the late 19th century', in Parret, 1976: 658–84.

Schmuck, Richard A. and Patricia A. Schmuck 1971, *Group Processes in the Classroom*, Dubuque, Iowa, Wm C. Brown.

Schumann, J.H. 1976, 'Second language acquisition: the pidginization hypothesis', *Language Learning* 26, 2, December: 391–408.

Schwartz, Joan 1980, 'The negotiation of meaning: repair in conversation between second language learners of English', in Larsen-Freeman, 1980: 138–53.

Scovell, Thomas 1979, Review of Lozanov, *Suggestology and Outlines of Suggestopedy*, *TESOL Quarterly* 13, 2, June: 255–66.

Searle, J. 1969, *Speech Acts*, Cambridge University Press.

Sebeok, Thomas A., Alfred S. Hayes and Mary Catherine Bateson (eds.) 1964, 'Approaches to Semiotics', *Transactions of the Indiana University Conference on Paralinguistics and Kinesics, 17–19 May 1962*, The Hague, Mouton.

Sharwood Smith, Michael 1981, 'Consciousness-raising and the second language learner', *Applied Linguistics* II, 2, Summer: 159–68.

Shaw, A.M. 1977, 'Foreign-language syllabus development: some recent approaches', *Language Teaching and Linguistics Abstracts* 10, 4, October: 217–33.

Shayer, David 1972, *The Teaching of English in Schools 1900–1970*, London, Routledge and Kegan Paul.

Simon, Herbert A. 1957, *Models of Man, Social and Rational*, New York, John Wiley.

Simon, Sidney B., L. Howe and Howard Kirschenbaum 1972, *Values Clarification: a Practical Handbook of Strategies for Teachers and Students*, New York, Hart.

Simons, Helen and Geoffrey Squires (compilers) 1976, *Small Group Teaching*, London, Group for Research and Innovation in Higher Education, The Nuffield Foundation.

Sinclair, J.McH. and R.M. Coulthard 1975, *Towards an Analysis of Discourse: the English Used by Teachers and Pupils*, Oxford University Press.

Skinner, B.F. 1957, *Verbal Behavior*, New York, Appleton-Century-Crofts. 1971, *Beyond Freedom and Dignity*, New York, Alfred A. Knopf.

Slavson, S.R. 1937, *Creative Group Education*, New York, Association Press.

Slobin, Dan Isaac 1979, *Psycholinguistics*, 2nd edn, Glenview, Ill., Scott Foresman and Co. (1st edn, 1971).

Smith, D.A. 1962, 'The Madras "snowball": an attempt to retrain 27,000 teachers of English to beginners', *English Language Teaching* 17, 1: 3–9.

Smith, Frank 1975, *Comprehension and Learning*, New York, Holt Rinehart and Winston.

Smith, Karl, David W. Johnson and Roger T. Johnson 1981, 'Can conflict be constructive? Controversy versus concurrence seeking in learning groups', *Journal of Educational Psychology* 73, 5, October: 651–63.

Smith, Larry E. (ed.) 1981, *English for Cross-Cultural Communication*, London, Macmillan.

Smith, Philip D. 1970, *A Comparison of the Cognitive and Audiolingual Approaches to Foreign Language Instruction: the Pennsylvania Foreign Language Project*, Philadelphia, Center for Curriculum Development.
1981, *Second Language Teaching: A Communicative Strategy*, Boston, Heinle and Heinle.

Spolsky, Bernard and Robert L. Cooper (eds.) 1977, *Frontiers of Bilingual Education*, Rowley, Mass., Newbury House.

Sprenger, Arnold 1973, 'Group work in foreign language learning: a report', *English Teaching Forum* XI, 5, November–December: 12–15.

Sprott, W.J.H. 1958, *Human Groups*, Harmondsworth, Penguin.

Stenhouse, Lawrence 1975, *An Introduction to Curriculum Research and Development*, London, Heinemann.

Stephenson, Norman and Denis Vincent (eds.) 1975, *Teaching and Understanding Drama*, Slough, National Foundation for Educational Research.

Stern, H.H. 1981, 'Communicative language teaching and learning: toward a synthesis', in Alatis, Altman and Alatis, 1981: 131–48.

Stern, H.H., Marjorie Bingham Wesche and Birgit Harley 1978, 'The impact of the language sciences on second language education', in Suppes, 1978: 397–475.

Stevick, Earl W. 1976, *Memory, Meaning and Method*, Rowley, Mass., Newbury House.
1980, *Teaching Languages: A Way and Ways*, Rowley, Mass., Newbury House.
1982, *Teaching and Learning Languages*, Cambridge University Press.

Stove, David 1982, *Popper and After: Four Modern Irrationalists*, Oxford, Pergamon Press.

Strauss, Wolfgang H. 1982, 'Problems of describing a specific terminology of foreign language methodology as a branch of social science', UNESCO, ALSED–LSP Newsletter 5, 1 (14), March, The Copenhagen School of Economics: 2–10.

Strevens, Peter 1977a, *New Orientations in the Teaching of English*, Oxford University Press.
1977b, 'Special-purpose language learning: a perspective', *Language Teaching and Linguistics Abstracts* 10, 3, July: 145–63.

Stubbs, Michael 1980, *Language and Literacy*, London, Routledge and Kegan Paul.

Sudnow, D. (ed.) 1972, *Studies in Social Interaction*, New York, Free Press.

Suppes, Patrick (ed.) 1978, *Impact of Research on Education: Some Case Studies*, Washington DC, National Academy of Education.

Sutherland, Kenton 1979, 'Accuracy vs. fluency in the English language classroom', *Cross Currents* 6, 2: 15–20.

Swain, Merrill 1972, 'Bilingualism as a First Language', unpublished Ph.D. dissertation, University of California, Irvine.

Swan, Michael 1981, 'False beginners', in Johnson and Morrow, 1981: 38–44.

Sweet, Paul R. 1980, *Wilhelm von Humboldt: a Biography*, Vol. 2, Columbia, Ohio State University Press.

Taba, Hilda 1962, *Curriculum Development*, New York, Harcourt Brace and World.

Tannen, Deborah 1981, 'Oral and literate strategies in spoken and written narratives', *Language* 58, 1, March: 1–21.

Tarone, Elaine 1979, 'Interlanguage as chameleon', *Language Learning* 29, 1, June: 181–92.

Terrell, Tracy D. 1977, 'A natural approach to second language acquisition and learning', *Modern Language Journal* LXI, 7, November: 325–36.

1982, 'The natural approach to language teaching: an update', *Modern Language Journal* 66, 2, Summer: 121–31.

Thelen, H.A. 1967, *Classroom Grouping for Teachability*, New York, Wiley.

Trudgill, Peter 1974, *Social Differentiation of English in Norwich*, Cambridge University Press.

Tulving, E. 1962, 'Subjective organization in free recall of "unrelated" words', *Psychological Review* 69, 4: 344–54.

Ullman, Rebecca 1981, 'A thematic and activity approach to communicative language teaching in second language classrooms', *Bulletin of the Canadian Association for Applied Linguistics* 3, 2, Autumn: 183–94.

Upshur, J.A. 1968, 'Four experiments on the relation between foreign language teaching and learning', *Language Learning* 18, 1 and 2, June: 111–24.

Vico, Giambattista 1981, *Selected Writings*, ed. Leon Pompa, Cambridge University Press.

Vygotsky, Lev Semenovich 1962, *Thought and Language*, ed. and trans. from Russian by Eugenia Haufmann and Gertrude Vakar, Cambridge, Mass., MIT Press (1st Russian edn, 1934).

Wales, R.J. and J.C. Marshall 1966, 'The organization of linguistic performance', in Lyons and Wales, 1966: 29–80.

Welford, A.T. 1968, *Fundamentals of Skill*, London, Methuen.

Wells, Gordon 1981, *Learning through Interaction*, Cambridge University Press.

Whewell, W. 1840, *The Philosophy of the Inductive Sciences*, London, John Parker.

White, John 1982, *The Aims of Education Restated*, London, Routledge and Kegan Paul.

White, R.V. 1980, *Teaching Written English*, London, Allen and Unwin.

Widdowson, H.G. 1968, 'The teaching of English through science', in Dakin, Tiffen and Widdowson, 1968: 115–75.

1975, 'EST in theory and practice', in *English for Academic Purposes*, ETIC Occasional Papers, London, The British Council: 1–13.

1978a, *Teaching Language as Communication*, Oxford University Press.

1978b, 'The significance of simplification', *Studies in Second Language Acquisition* 1: 11–20.

1978c, 'Notional–functional syllabuses, part iv', in Blatchford and Schachter, 1978: 33–5.

1979, *Explorations in Applied Linguistics*, Oxford University Press.

1980, 'Models and fictions', *Applied Linguistics*, I, 2, Summer: 165–70.

1981, 'Course design and discourse process', paper presented to Mextesol Convention, October.

1982, 'English as an international language: what do we mean by "international language" ', in Brumfit, 1982: 9–14.

1983, *Learning Purpose and Language Use*, Oxford University Press.

Widdowson, H.G. and C.J. Brumfit 1981, 'Issues in second language syllabus design', in Alatis, Altman and Alatis, 1981: 197–210.

Wigdorsky, Leopoldo 1972, 'Accuracy and fluency', *English Language Journal* 3, 1: 21–6.

Wilkins, D.A. 1972, 'Grammatical, situational and notional syllabuses', in AILA, 1972: 254–65, cited from Brumfit and Johnson, 1979: 82–90.

1976, *Notional Syllabuses*, Oxford University Press.

Wilkins, D.A., C.J. Brumfit and C. Bratt Paulston 1981, 'Notional syllabuses revisited, a response, some comments, and a further reply', *Applied Linguistics* II, 1, Spring: 83–100.

Winch, Peter 1958, *The Idea of a Social Science*, London, Routledge and Kegan Paul.

Winitz, Harris and James Reeds 1975, *Comprehension and Problem Solving as Strategies for Language Training*, The Hague, Mouton.

Wolfson, N. 1976, 'Speech events and natural speech', *Language in Society 5*, August: 189–209.

Index

Index of names